# Should Christians be Torah Observant?

## Carmen Welker

Printed in the United States of America

ISBN 978-1-934916-00-1

Unless otherwise indicated, all Bible references are from Stern's Complete Jewish Bible.

Second Edition, April 2008

NETZARI
PRESS

# Dedication

**This book is dedicated to** my very supportive husband without whom this project would not have been possible.  And to:

❖ Ellis Ipock who led me to the "right place at the right time" in January 1995 and was instrumental in "jump-starting" my glorious journey with God.

❖ Baruch ben Daniel for his comments and suggestions, and for graciously allowing me to incorporate some of his writings into this book.

❖ Andrew Gabriel Roth who allowed me unlimited permission to quote from his Netzari Aramaic English Interlinear and other writings.

# About the front cover

I chose for my book cover the menorah because it not only represents one of the oldest symbols of the Jewish faith but it is the **only** symbol YHWH, our Creator, designed Himself (Exodus 25:31-40). The menorah is also said to be a symbol of Israel's mission to be "a light unto the nations" (Isaiah 42:6).

Please note, the menorah on our front cover, made of pure 24k gold, was painstakingly made to look like the original in the First Temple. It is currently on display in The Cardo in Jerusalem in a protected Plexiglas room. Constructed by The Temple Institute of the Old City, it is the actual menorah that will be used when the Third Temple is built. For more information, please visit the Third Temple website: http://www.thirdtemple.com/OldCity/gallery.htm.

# Table of Contents

# Should Christians be Torah Observant?

# Prologue

## "Something" missing in the Church....

I was 44 years old before I finally found my way to God. It happened when the Holy Spirit grabbed hold of me one cold winter day in 1995, in a small country Baptist church in Missouri where the Pastor, Wil Pounds, just "happened" to say all the right things to make me realize I would be more than just worm fodder when I died.

The comments that actually pushed me "over the edge" went something like this: "Let's suppose for a moment you died today and stood before the Lord God and He asked you, 'Why should I let you into My heaven?' What would you say to Him? Would your response be something like, 'I am a religious person trying to live a Christian life the best I can'? Or, 'I go to church, give to the poor, help people in need, and have always tried to be a good person'?"

My eyes were wide as saucers as I contemplated Wil's question, and I quickly decided, "Yes, that's pretty much what my answer would be. What else could you say? What else is there?" But Wil's next comment knocked me for the proverbial loop, when he continued: "If your answer to any of these questions was 'yes' then you'd be wrong because NONE of those things would get you into heaven! The **only** thing that gets you into heaven is your belief in the shed blood at the cross – by faith in Jesus Christ who died on the cross paying the penalty for our sins...."

I was stunned! Until that day, I had never understood why anyone in their right mind would be willing to die a hideous death for the world at large, or how that particular death was supposed to affect my relationship with God. But when Wil's words hit home something inside me "clicked" and I realized for the first time in my life that Jesus was our FINAL SIN SACRIFICE; He was the divine Being who forever abolished the need for animal sin sacrifices God had always required of His people since the day Adam and Eve were evicted from the Garden!

As someone who was born Jewish in a tiny town in post-war Germany where God was basically dead, I knew next to nothing about the Bible and never really cared to; and so naturally I was taken aback over the things Wil was espousing. I had always "believed" in God and figured that, while He knew I was sinning, He forgave me because He also understood I was a mere human who had already been through hell on

Earth, and so He surely wouldn't condemn me there for eternity.

Yet, there I was in all my middle-aged glory, finally discovering that I had a Savior whose atoning death had relieved me of my need to hide from God anymore, or agonize over the willful things I had done to displease Him. Until then, I had been floundering around in my daily routine, trying to recover from a lifetime of endless trials and tribulations, and attempting to fill that "little hole in my soul" with worldly stuff....

In the following weeks after I "got saved" Pastor Wil began tutoring his new "baby Christian" relentlessly – and, of course, I was a virtual sponge, learning everything I possibly could from this amazing teacher. I faithfully completed all the workbooks he recommended and also attended Sunday school and evening Bible studies wherever I could find them. Over the course of about a year, I generally drove Wil crazy with non-stop questions, while he introduced me to a brand new world designed to show me what being "born again" was all about. I simply couldn't get enough of Jesus!

It wasn't long before I became Bible literate enough to begin asking some really tough questions. For instance, I quickly came to realize that the entire Bible was all about the Jews and Israel, and I became confused – not to mention worried – about the idea that my brethren would all go to hell because they didn't believe that Jesus was God. I remember wondering if the Jews (who already believed in the God of Abraham, Isaac and Jacob) were God's "Chosen People" then why would they end up in hell just because they didn't "believe in Jesus?" Did everybody BEFORE Jesus go to hell because they didn't have a chance to believe in Him? I mean, neither Enoch (Genesis 5:24) nor Elijah (2 Kings 2:11) "believed in Jesus" and yet they both went to heaven....

Eventually, I also began to wonder why the church felt that Jesus had "done away with the law" because, according to what I was gleaning from the Bible, "the law" was Torah, God's original **divine** teaching and instruction, outlined in the first five books of the Bible. The Books of Leviticus, Numbers and Deuteronomy go into agonizing detail on who God is, how He wants to be worshipped, the Feasts He wants us to celebrate (all of which foreshadow Jesus), how He wants us to behave, how He wants us to treat each other, and even what He wants us to eat. Without the Torah, we wouldn't have any of these guidelines which comprise our ONLY perfect blueprint for safe, moral and godly living – so why would God's original teachings and commands become null and void just because Jesus' human body died? Why would we WANT them to become null and void?

Throughout my "Baby Christian" days the Holy Spirit kept telling me that Jesus was our SIN Sacrifice, not someone who came to replace God the Father and His original teachings. After all, in Old Testament times, the animals that were killed to atone for man's sins covered our SINS only; their deaths didn't magically abolish any of God's commandments, so why would the death of His Son? **Covenants** changed, but God's Torah did not. The "New Testament" constantly refers to the "Old Testament" which contains all the original teachings and the "Thus saith the Lord" verses, not the other way around. It simply does not make any sense to insist that just because Jesus died, all of God's original teachings supposedly went out the window. It makes no sense to think the seventh day Sabbath which our Creator instituted and personally observed (Genesis 2:2) was changed to the first day, or that pork and shellfish somehow became "clean" just because Jesus died!

In Matthew 5:17 Jesus even said: *"Do **not** think that I came to abolish the Law or the Prophets; I did **not** come to abolish but to fulfill."* To me that indicated a beginning, not an ending or an "abolishing". If Jesus didn't "abolish" then "fulfill" could NOT mean "put an end to."

Something else that bothered me was the fact that the Church considers God's original teachings a "curse." How could anything God ever taught be a curse? If Torah is a curse, then why do both Isaiah and Micah tell us that "in the last days" Torah/the Law **will** be taught upon Jesus' return: *The law will go out from Zion, the word of the LORD from Jerusalem.* (NASB) Will we be living "under a curse" in the future when Jesus returns to rule and reign? If so, why is everyone so eager for "the Rapture?"

5

I also noticed that the Torah contains several "forever" commands, such as the Biblical Feasts which the Bible clearly states are to be observed FOREVER. But, whenever I asked a pastor or Bible study teacher about this, they always insisted that, as a Christian, I wouldn't have to worry about them because the "Old Testament" commands were directed only at the Jews. How could this be, I wondered, since we all worship the **same God** who had specifically instructed the "foreigners" and all who "attached themselves" to Israel to do **exactly** as the Jews (Numbers 15:13-16)? Shouldn't those tenets apply equally to everyone, or did God at some point hand down two different sets of rules?

Millions of questions raced through my mind and soon I began to feel that "something wasn't right" in the Church. Despite the fact that I was now "saved" I felt unfulfilled somehow, yet could not figure out why. Wherever I turned with my myriad questions, I ended up being hammered with the mantras, "The law is a curse" and "Jesus nailed it to the cross"....

For months, I studied everything I could get my hands on, eagerly soaking up the Bible, asking questions and mulling over certain Church teachings that didn't seem to make sense. For some reason I couldn't shake the nagging feeling that, although I had always "believed" in God on some level – this "Jesus" just didn't seem like the same God who had given Man His original teaching and instruction. Nothing against any of the pastors I have ever studied under and learned from, but what I thought I was reading in the Bible didn't exactly match what I was hearing from the podium....

For instance, the Gospels are clear that Jesus kept the seventh day Sabbath and the Biblical feasts as His Father commanded. I saw no place in the Bible that suggested those things had been done away with, even in the writings of Paul. As a matter of fact, unlike most people who seem to believe that Paul was against "the law," I personally felt that his writings had been misunderstood because I, even as a "baby Christian" could see clearly that Paul, like Jesus, was a Torah observant Jew who upheld the Law. He actually said so in Romans 3:31: *Do we then nullify the Law through faith? May it never be! On the contrary, we establish the Law.* (NASB) If we **establish** the Law, then we can't at the same time insist it's been abolished. Furthermore, 1 John 3 clearly says that sin is "lawlessness" – which means "the Law" could not have been abolished at the cross!

*1 John 3: 4 Everyone who sins breaks the law; in fact, sin is lawlessness. 5 But you know that he appeared so that he might take away our sins. And in him is no sin. 6 No one who lives in him keeps on sinning. No one who continues to sin has either seen him or known him.* (NIV)

And so I remained frustrated until God caused me to move to Colorado in 1996, where I eventually got the answers to all my questions after discovering "Messianic Judaism" – a belief based on the idea that the Bible is one, continuous, "God-breathed" entity as opposed to two, separate "testaments" wherein one supersedes the other.

Through some miraculous circumstances, I ended up in a Torah class learning things I could have never gleaned from a regular church setting. For instance, I learned that much of God's teaching and instruction has been mistranslated because of the intricacies of the Hebrew language, and that Paul's teachings have indeed been misunderstood because they are being viewed through a "Greek/Gentile" mindset. I learned that Jesus' given Hebrew Name was actually Yeshua, which means "Yahweh is Salvation." (Yeshua isn't that hard to pronounce in ANY language, and I wondered why "the world" had seen fit to change it.) Not only had His Name been changed, but also the dates of His birth, death and resurrection which are clearly outlined in the Bible! I also learned the difference between the "Hebrew" and the "Greek" mindsets which helped to clarify why "Jesus" in no way resembles the Torah observant, seventh day Sabbath and Feast keeping, kosher Jew who walked this Earth two thousand years ago....

And now, I want to pass this knowledge on to you. If, after you read the following pages you still don't believe that Christians should be Torah observant, at least you will be able to make up your mind from a more informed perspective. May God bless and enlighten you as you read the following pages.

# Chapter 1

## Torah is not "legalism" — it is the Word of God

*Matthew 7: 21 Not everyone who says to me 'Lord, Lord' will enter the Kingdom of Heaven, only those who do what my Father in heaven wants. 22 On that Day, many will say to me, 'Lord, Lord! Didn't we prophesy in your name? Didn't we expel demons in your name? Didn't we perform many miracles in your name?' 23 Then I will tell them to their faces, 'I never knew you! Get away from me, you workers of lawlessness!'*

Every believer owes it to him or herself to ask the question: "Am I really worshipping God according to what the Bible says, or am I blindly following Man? I mean, how do I know for sure that my particular denomination is the one God approves of, and whether or not we are 'doing it right'? "

The answer, of course, is: MAN came up with all the denominations and NONE of them are "doing it right!" Man with his limited human mindset has put God in a box and attempted to force Him to fit into the "theology du jour." Rather than to consult the Holy Spirit to help him understand God and the Bible, Man has picked his way through the Scriptures in search of whatever supports his particular premise. The result has been a myriad "denominations" (there are more than 1,500 Christian faith groups in North America alone) each claiming THEY are "the right" one....

It's no wonder then that, in recent years, many Christians have gone "church shopping" and/or completely exited the church altogether because they felt "something was missing." Some ultimately found themselves in "Messianic" congregations where a "whole new world" opened up when they discovered that what they had been missing was a working knowledge of Torah, the first five Books which contain God's original teachings; Torah, which foreshadows Yeshua who has so far only fulfilled the first four of the seven Biblical Feasts; Torah, without which Man would have **no** blueprint for moral behavior.

If you are among those Christians who have felt that certain "nudging" in your spiritual life, this book will serve as a true eye-opening experience, because you'll find that "Torah" is not what you thought! Torah is not "legalism" as the Church insists; it is the Word of God. Legalism consists of the **man-made** concepts which crept into Torah....Yet, many Christians are quick to point out that those who are Torah observant are "under the law" or practicing "legalism." Nothing could be further from the truth!

*James 4: 11 Brothers, stop speaking against each other! Whoever speaks against a brother or judges a brother is speaking against Torah and judging Torah.* **And if you judge Torah, you are not a doer of what Torah says, but a judge.** *12 There is but one Giver of Torah; he is also the Judge, with the power to deliver and to destroy. Who do you think you are, judging your fellow human being?*

Before we begin our study, I'd like to make it perfectly clear that this book is not intended to "bash" our Christian or Catholic brethren, nor does it advocate that Torah "saves" us; **only** the shed blood of Messiah has that power. I am also not suggesting that "Messianic" teachers have cornered the market on Truth because God knows Satan has infiltrated the "Messianic Movement" just as much as any other "religion." What I am attempting to get across is that believers in Christ must begin to read the Bible for what it actually says, and adhere to **God's** teachings instead of blindly swallowing whatever their respective priests or pastors espouse.

This book will demonstrate that Christians have misunderstood God's concept of "the Law" and, as a result, they are missing out on many blessings – not to mention, the "bigger picture" in the grand scheme of things – which includes the misleading "Jesus nailed it to the cross" idea that has caused many to confuse legalism (the traditions and opinions of men) with the actual commands of YHWH (transliteration of the Hebrew letters comprising our Creator's Name:

יהוה = Yud-Hey-Vav-Hey = YHWH, pronounced Yahweh).[1]

The bottom line is, we are living in the end times as outlined in the Books of Daniel and Revelation, and it is imperative that church leaders begin to re-examine their stance on whether or not they are teaching according to YHWH's instructions. By ignoring "the bigger picture" pastors all over the world are guilty of leading people astray – and their flocks are guilty of **allowing** themselves to be led astray!

This is not to imply that Christians (and Catholics and everyone else who believes in Jesus) don't "love the Lord." However, by ignoring Torah they are guilty of willfully disobeying some of YHWH's "forever" commands, which puts them in danger of being considered "lukewarm" on Judgment Day (Revelation 3:16), and consequently ending up the "least" in the Kingdom (Matthew 5:19).

Therefore, this book is going to make two bold suggestions (which will probably make more sense to you once you've finished reading it):

---

1 The letters YHWH were inspired by the Ruach haKodesh (Holy Spirit) to appear nearly 7,000 times in the Tanakh (Old Testament), yet the Name is nowhere to be found in our English versions except where it appears in an abbreviated form at the end of the word "Halleluyah." English translators were guilty of adding to our Creator's Word by replacing His personal Name with the capital letters LORD, GOD and the hybrid "Jehovah".

**Pastors:** Those pastors who desire to be accurate, on-the-mark stewards of YHWH's Word need to prayerfully reconsider what they were taught in seminary or other Christian settings, and re-examine the Bible with "new eyes" to see whether or not their teachings and actions line up with the Words of God – beginning with the rules, regulations, works and theologies of their own respective denominations (all of which were man-made).

**Congregations:** If pastors refuse to follow the example of Yeshua (our Savior's given, Hebrew Name which means "YHWH Saves" or "YHWH is Salvation"), our Torah observant, seventh day Sabbath and Feast keeping Savior, then their congregations have the responsibility to exit the churches, forget about what they've been taught and, with the help of the Holy Spirit, begin their own journeys into God's Word! Matthew 7:13 tells us that most people will NOT be entering through the "narrow gate that leads to life" and so it is imperative that you at least be able to make up your own mind about Torah from an **informed** perspective, before you decide to accept or reject it.

YHWH said: *My people are destroyed for want of knowledge....* (Hosea 4:6). To become the well-versed witness He wants you to be, you first need to figure out precisely what "knowledge" you have missed out on – starting with the fact that Christians who have been taught "Jesus nailed it to the cross" don't seem to understand exactly **what** was nailed to the cross. They are under the erroneous impression that this refers to God's original divine teachings, even though there is nothing in Scripture to substantiate this idea!

So, exactly what was "nailed to the cross"?

Yeshua "nailed to the cross" *the requirement to provide sacrifices to atone for our sins.* That is all. He did not come to replace YHWH the Father, nor did He ever suggest that He came to do away with His Father's rules and regulations nor any of the original teachings; on the contrary, He came to impress upon us the need to learn and obey the very Torah that He Himself observed and enforced!

Yeshua worked very hard to make us aware of the man-made concepts and ideologies that had crept into YHWH's Word, and to show us how to discern and weed out the endless barrage of rabbinical laws that kept in bondage the ancient believers. Ironically, today's Christian pastors are guilty of perpetuating their own "rabbinical" notions which include telling their congregations that "the law" was abolished, without even realizing they're talking about GOD's divine, eternal Laws!

As proof that "Jesus nailed it to the cross," however, pastors readily refer to the much mistranslated and misunderstood teachings of Paul which supposedly show that YHWH changed the seventh-day Sabbath to Sunday (the first day), render null and void the Biblical Feasts, and suggest Man can now eat pork and shellfish – and all this just because Yeshua died on the cross....

Why has hardly anyone questioned these supposed discrepancies or checked to see what the Bible actually says? How many have even noticed that Yeshua said He did **not** come to abolish Torah?

*Matthew 5: 17 "Don't think that I have come to abolish the Torah or the Prophets. I have come not to abolish but to complete. 18 Yes indeed! I tell you that until heaven and earth pass away,* **not so much as a yud or stroke will pass from the Torah – not until everything that must happen has happened.** *19 So whoever disobeys the least of these mitzvot (words/commands) and teaches others to do so will be called the least in the Kingdom of Heaven. But whoever obeys them and so teaches will be called great in the Kingdom of Heaven. 20 For I tell you that unless your righteousness is far greater than that of the Torah-teachers and P'rushim (prophets), you will certainly not enter the Kingdom of Heaven.*

Has everything happened that must happen? Have heaven and earth passed away? If not, then why is the Church ignoring Torah? How do the concepts of "complete or fulfill" equate to "abolished or done away with"?

And how in the world did intelligent people ever allow themselves to be talked into the arrogant, impudent and rebellious idea that God's Law could EVER be "a curse"? Or the belief that YHWH doesn't expect anything more of us than to "believe in Christ" while we're ignoring His commanded "forever" Feasts and instead, celebrating **man-made** "holy days" and traditions completely steeped in paganism?

15

Here's the sobering million dollar question: If you're among those who believe "the law is a curse," would you be willing to stake your eternal life on this philosophy without even bothering to take a second look at the Bible, just to make sure?

### Here's an example to illustrate Torah:

Good parents teach their children to obey some fundamental rules during their formative years. We teach them that touching a hot stove will burn their fingers, that trying to play with stray dogs might result in being bitten, or that it's dangerous to cross the street without first checking to see if a car is coming. We teach them necessary manners and show them how to get along with others, and to say "please" and "thank you"– basic rules of etiquette. The purpose of our careful tutelage is to raise decent human beings and to provide our offspring with knowledge they can carry with them forever; knowledge they can build on and eventually impart to their own kids. In other words, we give them a kind of "Torah"– a blueprint for moral and safe behavior.

Now, imagine, for instance, some flashy, charismatic person coming along and telling your children that whenever they reach the age of, say, 12, they will no longer be required to obey their parents and can do whatever they want, regardless of the consequences, because somehow the age of 12 magically negates everything their parents ever taught them. At age 12, according to this charismatic person, our children are "grown up" and no longer subject to their parents' rules and regulations. They can lie, steal, cheat, have sex whenever and with whomever they want, they can touch hot stoves, cross the road without looking, and generally do whatever they desire because, after all, you only live once. As humans who are born into sin (Genesis 3; Romans 3), our kids will naturally be drawn to this new liberty they think they've discovered, and so they begin to rebel because our rules and regulations are outdated and no longer accommodate their desires....

The problem is: Will our children's "new liberty" appeal to us parents? Of course not, because we know their actions will ultimately result in certain pain and/or death!

But isn't this exactly what we have done with the Word of YHWH by insisting "we are under grace" because "Jesus nailed it to the cross" and we're therefore not subject to God's Laws today? It seems only the rare Christian has ever demanded to know:

- Why would God decide to destroy or change His mind about His own original divine teachings, without which we would have no guide to moral life?

- Since Jesus said He came NOT to abolish but to fulfill Torah, what makes us think "fulfill" equated to "abolish"? Why are Christians ignoring the Biblical Feasts and the seventh day Sabbath commands – and how did His death on the cross as the

17

final Sin Sacrifice supposedly make YHWH change His mind about "clean" and "unclean" foods?

- Why do the teachings of Paul seem to contradict the teachings of Jesus – even though Paul was a Torah observant Jew who said that the Law was NOT abolished, but rather established or confirmed?

- Why are there so many and widely varying Christian denominations (not to mention, world "religions") each claiming to be "the right one"? What was YHWH's particular "religion" or denomination ?

- Why have so many Christian pastors over the years had to step down in shame from their self-indulgent pedestals for one reason or another? Weren't they doing God's will? And if not, why not? How come they were allowed to call themselves "men of the cloth" if they were off doing their own thing?

- Have we not "added to" Scripture by coining new terms such as "Trinity" and "Rapture" and celebrating the man-made "holy days" of Christmas and Easter – none of which can be found in the Bible? Since YHWH was so specific, right down to the smallest detail concerning His

Biblical Feasts, shouldn't we be celebrating them instead? Where in the Bible are we told Jesus abolished the Biblical Feasts, especially since He has so far only fulfilled the first four of the seven?

A favorite mantra of Christians is, "The law is written on our hearts!" Unfortunately, this is an untrue statement because, unless one has first LEARNED YHWH's Laws, one cannot have them "written on their hearts"....

Thanks to the willful disobedience of Adam and Eve in the Garden of Eden, mankind is automatically born into sin (Romans 3:10 and 3:23); and so, contrary to popular opinion, human babies are NOT born with God's Torah engraved upon their hearts. Just as they must be taught that hot stoves are dangerous, they must first be taught to memorize His do's and don'ts before ANYTHING is "written on their hearts."

The Apostle Paul who, as I've suggested has been much misunderstood by the Christian population (which this book will demonstrate later on), said:

*Romans 2: 12. For those without Torah, who sin, will also perish without Torah; and those under the Torah, who sin, will be judged by the Torah. 13.* **For not the hearers of the Torah are righteous before Elohim; but the doers of the Torah** *are being made righteous. 14. For if Gentiles who have not the Torah shall, by their nature, do the things of the Torah; they, while without the Torah,* *become a Torah to themselves. 15. Additionally, they show the work of the Torah as it is inscribed on their hearts; and their conscience bears testimony to them, their own reflections rebuking or vindicating one another. 16. (And that vindication is for) in the day in which Elohim will judge the secret [actions] of men, as my tidings [teaches], by Y'shua the Mashiyach.* (From the Netzari Aramaic English Interlinear by Andrew Gabriel Roth)

Please ask the Ruach haKodesh (Holy Spirit) to help you understand Romans 2:12-16 above, which was translated directly from Aramaic into English. It does not in any way infer that Christians don't need the Torah, but rather that, without divine guidance, they will make up their own rules and regulations and attempt to decipher "right from wrong" and "rebuke and vindicate" each other from a human standpoint.

A footnote from Roth's Netzari Aramaic English Interlinear referring to this scripture, says: "Paul does not suggest that Gentiles should spontaneously master the Torah. The point is they should learn the written Torah without distraction from Pharisaic traditions which are not rooted in the plain understanding of Torah."

At the beginning of this chapter, I used Matthew 7:21-23, which discusses how YHWH will reject the "workers of lawlessness." We need to honestly ask ourselves: Who are the "workers of lawlessness"? Answer: Those who don't conform to God's Laws! It's hypocritical to think of ourselves as "saints" while we are guilty of willful and deliberate sinning through our refusal to conform to Elohim's Laws. According to the Merriam-Webster Dictionary sin is the "transgression of the law of God" (1 John 3:4). Willfully ignoring Torah is breaking God's Laws, simple as that.

As Scripture affirms in several places, there is but **one** YHWH and **one** divine Instruction for the Jew and for the foreigner who has chosen to follow the God of Abraham, Isaac and Jacob. Isra'el was to be the example for all other nations to follow, not the sole user of the Torah.

Torah is our relationship to God; it reveals who He is, how He wants to be worshipped, and how He wants us to live and behave according to what He knows is best for us. (And, as all good, God-fearing Christians should know, if we desire to have a relationship with God, we cannot pick and choose what we want to believe of the Bible! We must either accept all or none of it....)

The following pages will demonstrate how Christians, as a whole, are missing the "big picture" – and consequently, losing out on some of YHWH's blessings because they are ignoring Torah and adhering instead to the watered-down gospel started by the "Church fathers" who passed off as Truth their twisted understanding of the "Old Testament" and the teachings of our Savior, Yeshua haMashiyach (Jesus Christ).

The prophet Micah asked:

*Micah 6: 6 "With what can I come before ADONAI to bow down before God on high?"*

I'm going to ask you to keep that verse in mind as you read through the pages of this book, and by the time you're done, you'll have a very good idea as to what you can bring before ADONAI....

# Chapter 2

## Origin of the "Torah was nailed to the cross" idea

There are plenty of "scholars" in this world who insist that Torah was only for the Jews and that anyone who belongs to Christ doesn't have to do anything but "believe." But what does the BIBLE say?

To find out, all we need to do is to go back to the origin of the "Torah was nailed to the cross" myth – which was started by the "Church fathers"– men who basically claimed for their own the God of Abraham, Isaac and Jacob, and then, intentionally and/or unintentionally, stripped Him of His true, Biblical identity! This happened, in part, because they hated the Jews and anything Jewish, and because they, as Gentiles, viewed YHWH and the Bible through a Greek instead of a Hebrew mindset.

What is meant by "Hebrew mindset" vs. "Greek mindset"? It refers to the idea that there is a discrepancy between the Jewish and Christian concepts about life, God and Truth; in other words, they were "set" in their respective ways of thinking about these issues. In the mindset of the Hebrews, YHWH was the Creator. Period. Greeks, on the other hand, were Gentiles prone to be atheistic, agnostic, or into pagan gods – and that's why the Apostle Paul used different methods when he spoke to the Hebrew and Greek cultures.

Example: The "Greek" mindset visualizes a tattoo (or something similar) on the thigh of Jesus when he returns as "King of Kings, and Lord of Lords" (Revelation 19:11-13, 16), while the Hebrew mindset sees something deeper, more realistic, more Torah-based. The Hebrew mindset visualizes Yeshua, the Torah observant Jewish Messiah wrapped in a tallit (prayer shawl) as He sits atop a white horse, headed back to Earth with the tzit-tzits (braids, knots, tassels) that fall across His thighs spelling out the Name of YHWH. (Each letter of the Hebrew alphabet has a numerical value and, consequently, the number of knots on the tzit-tzits on the four corners of a tallit, tied properly, spell out the name of YHWH. No tattoo required!)

Another example of a Hebrew as opposed to Greek mindset can be seen in the respective calendars/timelines. YHWH's timelines are amply evidenced throughout the Bible, whereas our Gregorian calendars are speckled with the names of pagan deities representing the days and months. According to YHWH, a "day" is **not** from midnight to midnight, but from "sunset to sunset" (Genesis 1:5). He called the days of the week the "first day," "second day," etc., whereas "the world" has named its days and months after pagan gods and goddesses.

Even though we're used to these names, we must search our hearts and be very honest with ourselves when posing the question: Since YHWH adamantly warned people about paganism and even put people to death for inserting anything unusual into our worship of Him (i.e., as in the case of Aaron's sons), why would He be happy about it today?

Anyway, the end result of these two different mindsets was devastating because, due to their misinterpretation, mistranslation, misunderstanding and misapplication of the Scriptures, Gentile church leaders managed to twist the Word of God and insert their own opinions into the equation. And their followers, of course, blindly accepted their "truth" as gospel. Down through the ages, rather than to examine the Bible and Messiah Yeshua's teachings for themselves, people continued to adhere to the teachings of the "Church fathers" without question, thus helping to perpetuate the "law is a curse" myth.

The following illustrations will give you a rough idea as to how the "Church fathers" influenced future generations of believers:

## The devil made us do it!

Luke 4 tells us that Satan knocked himself out to tempt Yeshua. When that failed (despite the promise of all the kingdoms in the world), Satan basically went for humankind's collective jugular, beginning with the insertion of false doctrine into the teachings of Yeshua; the main one being that "Christians" didn't need to be Torah observant.

The fact is, however, the Bible clearly shows that early Gentile believers **were** Torah observant – yet most Christians will adamantly refute this, using everything in their power to prove otherwise, and always presenting as their "indisputable proof" the misinterpreted teachings of Paul.

But please take a look at scriptures such as 1 Corinthians 5:8 where Paul, speaking of the Feast of Passover during which we are to rid ourselves of the leaven in our houses, says: "So let us celebrate the Seder"....(Some versions say, "keep the festival" or "celebrate the feast" which refers directly to Passover!)    Paul said to celebrate Passover, not "Easter."   Passover is one of the Feasts outlined in Torah (Exodus 12, Leviticus 23:4, Numbers 9).

Also, Acts 13:42-44 clearly shows that Gentiles in Antioch requested further instruction of Paul "on the next Sabbath" (YHWH's Sabbath is and always has been Saturday/the seventh day) and that almost the whole city arrived for the meeting on the next Sabbath. There were never any separate Sunday (first day) "Sabbath" meetings.  In Yeshua's time on Earth both Jews and Gentiles regularly attended the synagogue for worship on the **seventh** day.

Why were those early believers willing to go along with the seventh day Sabbath? (I use the term "believers" rather than "Christians" because Christianity didn't come into being until after 100 A.D.) It's because YHWH said that His Sabbath was on the seventh day (Genesis 2:1-3), and He had commanded that anyone who worshipped Him was to do **exactly** as the Jews:

*Numbers 15: 13 "***Every citizen** *is to do these things in this way when presenting an offering made by fire as a fragrant aroma for ADONAI.  14 If a foreigner stays with you – or whoever may be with you, through all your generations – and he wants to bring an offering made by fire as a fragrant aroma for ADONAI,* **he is to do the same as you***.  15 For this community there will be* **the same law** *for you as for the foreigner living with you; this is a* **permanent regulation through all your generations;** *the foreigner is to be treated the same way before ADONAI as yourselves.  16* **The same Torah and standard of judgment will apply to both you and the foreigner living with you.***'"*

Throughout the Bible one can find absolutely no evidence that YHWH or Yeshua **ever** claimed the first day as holy or blessed in any way.  As a matter of fact, we read that Moses told Isra'el in the wilderness on the sixth day of the week, *"Tomorrow is a holy Shabbat (Sabbath) for ADONAI…"* (Exodus 16:23; also see Isaiah 56:2-7).

When early Gentiles accepted the Good News of Messiah Yeshua they unhesitatingly became Torah observant. History books reveal that, by the end of the First Century A.D., the number of Gentile believers outnumbered Jewish believers (obviously because there were, and still are, more Gentiles in the world than Jews). But ultimately, because some Gentile believers had limited understanding of the Hebrew roots of their faith and of YHWH's eternal covenant with Isra'el (Romans 11:1-2), they began to veer off to form a separate religion that set in motion a "de-Judaizing process" which departed from Yeshua's original teachings.

Eventually, when Gentile Christianity emerged as the dominant faith in "Jesus," it suddenly became taboo for Jews to believe in the Torah observant Messiah Yeshua and, in order to "believe" they had to covert to the Torah-less Christianity! The time came when they were actually killed for refusing "Jesus"! Can you blame most Jews today for not wanting any part of Him? They've been driven away by the paganism that Man has incorporated into their Creator's teachings!

Even today Christians still approach Jews to admonish them that if they don't stop "being under the law" and start "believing in Jesus" (who in no way resembles the Jewish Messiah who walked upon this Earth), they are going to hell – never mind that Torah observant Jews ALREADY have an unparalleled relationship with YHWH that puts to shame any other "religious denomination"!

**Back to the "Church fathers"....**

28

Due to their limited understanding of the Jewish God and Hebrew concepts, the early "Church fathers" were extremely instrumental in changing our perception of YHWH and His Son. They twisted Scriptures and inserted their own opinions; changed our Savior's Name to "Jesus" (the letter J wasn't even around until the Fifteenth Century); changed his birthday from the first day of Sukkot/Feast of Tabernacles to December 25th (never mind the fact that YHWH never said to concentrate on His birthday at all); and they suggested He abolished YHWH's Torah including the seventh-day Sabbath and the Biblical Feasts, as those holy days were meant "only for Jews." (Same God, different rules? How does that make sense?) And, despite the fact that YHWH commanded us not to have idols or to make graven images, they placed statues of Jesus (and Mary) in every Catholic church and hung Him on the cross in many Christian churches! Never mind that no one has actually seen Him face-to-face in two thousand years and is able to proclaim that today's statues are a true representation of our Savior....

As an added slap in the face of God, the Catholics and Christians decided that "the Jews" were the "bad guys" and when they weren't harassing, imprisoning or slaughtering Jews in the Inquisition, the pogroms or the Holocaust, Church leaders were teaching that Judaism had been replaced with a new religion that had new rules which, of course, in no way bore any resemblance to Judaism! How could this have been possible since Christians worshipped the same God as the Jews – the God whom the Bible said was the same today, yesterday and forever (Hebrews 13:8)?

Be that as it may, "Church founders" such as Ignatius (35-107 CE), Marcion (110-160 AD) and Tertullian (155-230 CE) were instrumental in tweaking the Scriptures and inserting their own opinions – which were immediately swallowed by "the world" as "true Gospel" seeking to free the Church from "false Jewish doctrines."

The following information about the early Church fathers was borrowed, with permission, from author and Aramaic scholar Andrew Gabriel Roth and his colleague Baruch ben Daniel, from an appendix in their Netzari Aramaic English Interlinear:

- **Ignatius** was considered to be an "auditor " and "disciple" of John who pioneered the Greek-based Christian religion and was instrumental in the assimilation of paganism into early Christianity, packaging Christianity for a Greco-Roman Hellenic culture. Ignatius saw Jewish followers of Y'shua as nothing more than legalists and Judaizers. He despised the observance of Shabbat (Sabbath) in favor of his Ishtar (Easter) sunrise "Lord's day" Sun-Day teachings. It is scarcely possible to exaggerate the importance of the Ignatian letters to modern Christian institutions as Ignatius was a key player in the development of the modern Christian church, promoting the "infallibility of the church" and the "universal church" which had incorporated large doses of paganism. If there ever was a hierarchy loving "Christian" with a Hellenistic autocratic mindset, it was Ignatius who gave himself the nickname Theophoros (the God-bearer) and taught that deacons, presbyters and bishops were a separate category of people, high and lifted up, and infused with Jesus-like authority to be lords over people. Christians consider Ignatius as one of the all time biggest movers and shakers of the all-Gentile church. He strongly instructed that "without the bishop's supervision, no baptisms or love feasts are permitted." He also believed Mary to be the eternal virgin mother of God.

- **Tertullian:** One of Tertullian's better known "achievements" was to fall into a trance and then prophesy under the influence of the "Holy Spirit" insisting his utterances were the voice of the "Holy Spirit." (The modern day tongues speaking "born again" Pentecostal or Charismatic Christians probably appreciate someone like Tertullian!) While fumbling in all manner of paganism and spiritism, Tertullian picked up an "anointing" of the "Holy Ghost" and coined the word "Trinity" which is one of the most beloved doctrines of the Church to this very day (more on this in a later chapter). The "persons of the trinity" doctrine flourishes in the hierarchy-based religion which sees itself as a three-sided pyramid structure. Tertullian's works abound with puns, wit, sarcasm and a continual pounding of his opponents with invectives.

- **Marcion:** Every Christian who uses the term "Old" and "New" testament must take their hats off to Marcion as he was the one who coined these terms which perfectly reflect the Hellenistic mindset of the pagan world which is ignorant of Torah. Marcion taught that the Old and New Testaments could not be reconciled with each other, and this is what we hear in Christian churches today.

Let's examine some of the writings of these early "Church fathers" beginning with Marcion, who taught the following:

1. Moses' form of law was "eye for an eye," and that Jesus reversed this.

2. Elisha caused bears to devour the little children, but Jesus said, "let the little children come to me."

3. Joshua stopped the sun in its path to continue a slaughter of the enemy, but

Paul said, "don't let the sun go down on your wrath."

4. The "Old Testament" permitted divorce and polygamy; but the "New Testament" denies both.

5. Moses enforced the Jewish Sabbath and Law, but Jesus freed believers from both.

6. God commanded that no work be done on the Sabbath, yet he told the Israelites to carry the ark around Jericho seven times on the Sabbath.

7. Graven images were prohibited by the Ten Commandments, yet Moses was instructed to fashion a bronze serpent.

8. The God of the Old Testament could not have been omniscient; otherwise he would not have asked, "Adam where are you?" (Genesis 3:9)

9. The God of the Old Testament was a ruthless God of vengeance, cruelty and wrath, but Jesus was full of grace and compassion.

10. Coined the terms "Old and New Testament."

## Here are the actual Biblical meanings:

1. "Eye for eye" is an idiomatic legal term meaning to render equivalent restitution. It does not in any way suggest physical punishment of the same. The value of the eye, ear, nose, arm must be restored by the person who injured it.

2. Elisha cursed the mocking children in Name of YHWH. As a result 42 were torn apart by two female bears. The number 42 represents disaster towards those who turn against YHWH. There were 42,000 Ephraimites slain in Judges 12:6; 42 relatives of Ahaziah were killed by Jehu in 2 Kings 10:14. According to Revelation 11:2 the Gentiles wreak havoc and do all manner of blasphemy for 42 months, and because there is a connection between the number 42 and the Name of the Most High; this may be referring to the Gentiles forcing the world to bow down to their Jesus god, at pain of death. While this in itself is nothing new, YHWH puts a permanent end to them by raising up His two witnesses. Elisha raised up a child from the dead and showed his great compassion for children in other places in Scripture. By viewing the Tanakh (the Jewish Bible which Christians refer to as the "Old Testament") through a Greek instead of a Hebrew mindset, Marcion, humanism

and false Christianity are not judging Elisha, but YHWH!

3. Joshua would have a tough time "stopping the sun" on his own strength. Joshua 10:11-13 records how more people died when YHWH sent down hailstones on them, than those who Joshua's armies slew. Joshua is Yehoshua, the same name as Y'shua; he is a type of Mashiyach. Marcion and false Christianity are judging YHWH and overruling YHWH's Sovereign authority and His Word (Torah) with their own injustice system. In reality, Christians have killed more people in the name of their religion, than ancient Israelites whom YHWH instructed to "destroy their altars, break their images, and cut down their groves (statues)," which was so Isra'el wouldn't be tempted to sacrifice unto the pagan gods or make molten gods (Shemot/Exodus 34:12-17). *"And if the people of the land do any ways hide their eyes from the man, when he gives of his seed unto Molech, and kill him not: Then I will set my face against that man, and against his family, and will cut him off, and all that go a whoring after him, to commit whoredom with Molech, from among their people."* (Vayikra/Leviticus 20:4-5). At Petra, Jordan, archeologists have found evidence of pagan rituals where the pagans cut the hearts out of young living children and while still

beating they sacrificed them and the blood to the sun deity. That is why YHWH commanded them to be wiped off the face of the earth. Those who have a problem with this, are willfully ignorant of the intent of YHWH's Commandments. But, before Mashiyach returns, YHWH will sanctify the Earth and establish His government. And finally, the hailstones in Joshua 10:11 remind us of Sodom and Gomorrah, which couldn't have been popular with Marcion and friends who lived in a culture where sodomy was commonplace.

4. Moshe (Moses) permitted divorce, but most Christians are ignorant of the process and consequences of obtaining release from a marriage covenant, whereas the John 8 fallacy of the woman caught in adultery showed no consequences for adultery. In terms of polygamy YHWH states in D'varim/Deuteronomy 17:17 that "you shall not multiply wives."

5. The Shabbat was given by YHWH at the Creation of the world. Mashiyach and all the Shlichim (apostles) observed Shabbat and brought Gentiles into the synagogues on Shabbat, to learn about the Kingdom of Elohim. The assimilation of a pagan

culture into Christianity changed worship from Shabbat to Sunday.

6. We are not told that the seven days began on the first day of the week (Sunday); therefore, one cannot assume that the seventh day at Jericho was also a weekly Shabbat. The Israelites had just observed Pesach (Passover); therefore, the seven day cycle round Jericho may have started on the first day of Chag haMatzah. The book of Jasher states that YHWH spoke to Joshua on the first day of the second month – again, this would not necessarily be on the first day of the week. Marcion's assumption is simply an attempt to judge YHWH's authority. YHWH gave the command to march, and YHWH pulled down the walls of Jericho. It seems Marcion had an evil imagination.

7. The bronze serpent on the pole was the antidote to the venom of the snake; those who looked to the bronze serpent were saved. Those who look to the suffering servant on the pole are saved from the bite of the serpent haSatan. Marcion willfully chose to forget that they weren't worshipping the serpent, yet he judges YHWH's Word and Authority as being flawed.

8. Marcion apparently couldn't appreciate that YHWH in His mercy gave Adam and

Eve a moment to compose themselves after they had transgressed.

9. Marcion's father was a bishop of the Christian church; therefore, Marcion was simply taking more steps to define Christianity as a religion based on Hellenism.

10. By replacing the word "Covenant" with "Testament," Greek theologians tried to wrestle Jeremiah 31:31-34 away from the teachings of Y'shua and the Shlichim and divide Y'shua away from his Father YHWH, into their own self sustained Jesus deity.

In view of what you have just read, you can surely see that the "Church fathers" were definitely guilty of "tweaking" and/or downright twisting the Scriptures. Some would argue that, while there might have been a slight problem with semantics, it isn't really that big of a deal.

But, if it really isn't that big a deal, then perhaps we need to look at it another way: If someone were to bake a batch of homemade cookies with just a tiniest bit of cow dung mixed into the dough, would you eat them – even though there was just a smidgeon of cow dung mixed into the entire batch? Of course you wouldn't! So, why are you willing to accept misunderstanding, misinterpretation and paganism to corrupt the perfect Word of God?

# Chapter 3

### And now, back to the Torah....

In light of the information contained within the first two chapters, can you begin to see why we need to ask the question: Why would Yeshua's death on the stake suddenly abolish YHWH's original Divine instructions or negate His "forever" commands?

In Biblical times the people at least had a valid excuse to "go astray": They blindly followed their rabbis because they couldn't read!  But today's believers cannot make that same claim, so why are people **still** blindly following the writings of the Church fathers or their respective congregation leaders, and allowing themselves to be sent down a path that has led them completely away from Biblical Truth?  Why are they not reading God's Word for themselves and speaking up when something seems "off"?

This would be a good place to ask:  Have you ever wondered why there are so many and varying Christian denominations, each claiming to be "the right one"? The answer is: Because they are all adhering to **half** the Bible and ignoring YHWH's actual teachings! They've totally ignored the very teachings that reveal exactly who He is, how He desires to be worshipped, and how we are to treat each other according to HIS desires. That's like starting in the middle of a novel without bothering to understand what happened in the first half. (And this refers just to Christianity; I'm not even talking about the myriad man-made "religions" that abound in the world which don't even acknowledge YHWH as Creator at all! They'll have their own "crosses to bear" on Judgment Day....)

Regardless, there ARE thousands of denominations and most Christians are quick to point out that Jeremiah 31 says God promised us a new covenant built on "grace" and therefore, all that is required to get into Heaven is to "believe in Jesus." The question is, since when does grace include permission to ignore YHWH's commands, His Torah?

In reading the "fine print" of Jeremiah 31:30 (verse 31 in some versions) we discover that the "New Covenant" was NOT made with the Gentiles nor any religious denomination, but with the Houses of **Isra'el** and **Judah** only:

*Jeremiah 31: 30(31) "Here, the days are coming," says ADONAI, "when I will make a new covenant with the house of Isra'el and with the house of Y'hudah.*

Please note YHWH did not make a "new covenant" with the Gentiles because He did not have an "old covenant" with the Gentiles! He did, however, extend His grace and mercy to the Gentiles who, once they become believers in Yeshua, automatically become part of Isra'el!

*Romans 11: 16 "… And if the root (Isra'el) is holy, so are the branches. 17 But if some of the branches were broken off, and you (Gentile) – a wild olive – were grafted in among them and have become equal sharers in the rich root of the olive tree, 18 then don't boast as if you were better than the branches! However, if you do boast, remember that you (Gentile) are not supporting the root (Isra'el), the root is supporting you. 19 So you will say, 'Branches were broken off so that I might be grafted in.' 20 True, but so what? They were broken off because of their lack of trust. However, you (Gentile) keep your place only because of your trust (in the Messiah)."*

And God told Isra'el:

*Proverbs 4: 2 "For I have given you a good teaching; do not forsake My Torah!"* (Stone Edition of the Tanakh)

The Netzari Aramaic English Interlinear clears up the misconception regarding the "new covenant" in Jeremiah 31:31-34 by explaining Hebrews 8:

> *Hebrews 8:10. But this is the covenant which I will give to the family of the house of Israel after those days, says Master YHWH: I will put my Torah in their minds and inscribe it on their hearts; and I will be to them a Elohim, and they shall be to me a people. 11. And one shall not teach his son of the city nor his brother, nor say: Know you Master YHWH: because they shall all know me, from the youngest of them to*

*the oldest. 12. And I will forgive them their iniquity;*
*and their sins will I remember no more. 13. In that*
*he said a New (Covenant), he made the first old; and*
*that which is old and decaying, is near to*
*disappearing.*

The context is Jeremiah 31:31-34; what is
"near to disappearing" is the sinful nature of
man that breaks Torah, not the standard of
Torah. Remember that **we** broke Torah, not
YHWH. YHWH did not drop the standard of
Torah because Israel chose disobedience;
rather, He installed a Renewed Covenant to
write Torah upon the heart through the work
of the Ruach haKodesh, according to
Mashiyach. The fact of the matter is that in
Mashiyach, YHWH raised the bar; He
magnified Torah, see Isaiah 42:21. Because
mankind broke the Covenant, YHWH
requires complete renovation on our part, not
YHWH's part of the Covenant. This verse in
its twisted form, became one of the "crown
jewels" of Torahless Christianity which
teaches that Torah is decaying and near to
disappearing, but nothing could be farther
from the truth. See 2 Peter 3:16.

Returning to the subject of covenants, let's briefly
discuss the intricacies of YHWH's treaties with His
creation:

Throughout the Bible we can see that YHWH's
covenants, although modified according to His will,
were never negated, abolished or replaced. For

instance, let's examine what happened when we received the "New Covenant":

The *covenant* changed, but the following did NOT:

- Torah
- YHWH's provisions
- The penalty for disobedience
- YHWH's promises

What DID change?

**The Steward:** Yeshua is now the steward, releasing Moses of that responsibility, which fulfills the prophecy of Deuteronomy 18:

*Deuteronomy 18: 18 "I will raise up for them a prophet like you from among their kinsmen; I will put my words in his mouth, and he will tell them everything I order him. 19 Whoever doesn't listen to my words, which he will speak in my name, will have to account for himself to me.*

**The Torah written on our hearts:** The Torah is presented and managed (not replaced – YHWH never said He was replacing Torah!) under a new covenant which is written on our hearts via the Ruach haKodesh (Holy Spirit), which fulfills the prophecy of Jeremiah 31:

*Jeremiah 31: 32 "For this is the covenant I will make with the house of Isra'el after those days," says ADONAI. "I will put my Torah within them and write it on their hearts; I will be their God, and they will be my people."*

Please note that "Torah written on our hearts" means we are willing to follow YHWH's instruction and learn and obey Torah; NOT that we are born with an innate knowledge about His teachings and commands which we can ignore at will!

**The priest:** Instead of an Aaronic high priest, the high priest is one "after the order of Melchizedek" – Yeshua our Messiah; which fulfills the prophecy of Psalm 110 in which King David wrote:

*Psalms 110: 1 ADONAI says to my Lord, "Sit at my right hand, until I make your enemies your footstool." 2 ADONAI will send your powerful scepter out from Tziyon, so that you will rule over your enemies around you. 3 On the day your forces mobilize, your people willingly offer themselves in holy splendors from the womb of the dawn; the dew of your youth is yours. 4 ADONAI has sworn it, and he will never retract – "You are a cohen forever, to be compared with Malki-Tzedek."*

**The sacrifice:** Innocent animals were sacrificed under the Mosaic covenant. But, under the new covenant, Yeshua Himself is the Sacrifice, thus fulfilling the foreshadowing of Psalm 40, which relates to animal sacrifice:

*Psalm 40: 7 Sacrifices and grain offerings you don't want; burnt offerings and sin offerings you don't demand. Instead, you have given me open ears; 8 so then I said, "Here I am! I'm coming! In the scroll of a book it is written about me. 9*

*Doing your will, my God, is my joy; your Torah is in my inmost being.*

We need to remember, as Paul said, Yeshua was our final SIN offering, and the **only** way to obtain eternal life is to believe in His shed blood on the cross. We find that eternal life is knowing God and knowing Yeshua (John 17:3). We "know God by obeying His commands. But when Torah observant believers talk about "walking in Torah" and keeping the feasts, however, people jump to conclusions and accuse of us doing it in order to receive eternal life; this is absolutely **not** true. Man is not "saved" by works! We cannot work or pray our way into heaven. But, we must keep Torah because YHWH commanded it; and because we want to (once it is written on our hearts); and because God never "did away with" His original instructions in Righteousness!

## So, what exactly is Torah?

To explain what Torah is, let's start with what it isn't:

Torah isn't legalism (man's requirements).

Torah isn't "the law" which was supposedly abolished on the cross, according to Christian understanding; but, rather, Torah comprises God's original teaching and instruction; His "do's" and "don'ts"; His blueprint for moral living. This blueprint, as mentioned earlier, is contained within the first five books of the Bible: Genesis, Exodus, Leviticus, Numbers, and Deuteronomy, also called the "Pentateuch"– and can be found in several "forever" verses, including 2 Chronicles 7:14-22 which shows that YHWH commanded believers to **keep His original teachings forever**:

*2 Chronicles 7: 14 "...then, if my people, who bear my name, will humble themselves, pray, seek my face and turn from their evil ways, I will hear from heaven, forgive their sin and heal their land. 15 Now my eyes will be open and my ears will pay attention to the prayer made in this place. 16 For now I have chosen and consecrated this house, so that my name can be there forever; my eyes and heart will always be there. 17 As for you, if you will live in my presence, as did David your father, doing everything I have ordered you to do, and keeping my laws and rulings; 18 then I will establish the throne of your rulership, as I covenanted with David your father when I said, 'You will never lack a man to be ruler in Isra'el.' 19 But if you turn away and abandon my regulations and mitzvot which I have set before you, and go and serve other gods, worshipping them; 20 then I will pull them up by the roots out of the land I have given them. This house, which I consecrated for my name, I will eject from my sight; and I will make it an example to avoid and an object of scorn among all peoples. 21 This house, now so exalted - everyone passing by will be shocked at the sight of it and will ask, 'Why has Adonai done this to this land and to this house?' 22 But the answer will be, 'It's because they abandoned Adonai the God of their ancestors, who brought them out of the land of Egypt, and took hold of other gods, worshipping and serving them; this is why Adonai brought all these calamities on them'."*

Today's Christians are included among the "foreigners" who love the God of Abraham, Isaac and Jacob! YOU are a part of Isra'el! According to Galatians 3:27-29, believers are "one in Messiah"–

"the seed of Abraham!" But yet, most have chosen to ignore (or at the very least, have forgotten, or talked themselves out of) the fact that Yeshua, the Savior YHWH sent to Earth as "God Incarnate" was revealed in the flesh as a Torah-observant, Sabbath and feast-keeping, kosher Jew!

*John 10: 30 I and the Father are one.*

How much clearer could this have been stated? Yeshua and the Father are ONE. YHWH is the same yesterday, today and forever (Hebrews 13:8), so why would He have sent His Son as a Torah observant Jew if not as an example for us to follow? When did YHWH ever indicate that Torah would be "nailed to the cross" or that it was to be considered a "curse" after Yeshua's death, as most Christians today insist?

God's blueprint for moral living and behavior was not given as a temporary thing. He clearly stated that His people would be recognized by their obedience to His "forever" commands – because those permanent ordinances are what set believers apart from the rest of the world, and from pagan religions. Let's review just a few examples of some of God's "forever" statutes:

Concerning the land of Isra'el belonging to Abraham and his descendants:

*Genesis 13: 15 All the land you see I will give to you and your descendants* **forever**....

Referencing the feast of Passover:

*Exodus 12: 24 You are to observe this as a law, you and your descendants* **forever**.

Concerning the Biblical feasts and the seventh-day Sabbath:

*Exodus 31: 12 ADONAI said to Moshe, 13 "Tell the people of Isra'el, 'You are to observe my Shabbats (feasts); for this is a sign between me and you* **through all your generations***; so that you will know that I am ADONAI, who sets you apart for me. 14 Therefore you are to keep my Shabbat (seventh-day Sabbath), because it is set apart for you. Everyone who treats it as ordinary must be put to death; for whoever does any work on it is to be cut off from his people.*

*Leviticus 23: 2 "Tell the people of Isra'el: 'The designated times of ADONAI which you are to proclaim as holy convocations are my designated times.*

Again: Who are "the people of Isra'el"? Anyone who follows the God of Abraham, Isaac, and Jacob! It cannot be emphasized enough that, as a grafted in Christian believer YOU are to be Torah-obedient, YOU are to eat kosher, and YOU are to keep the seventh day Sabbath and the Biblical feasts – all of which foreshadow Yeshua, who has so far only fulfilled the first four of the seven! (More on that later.)

*Exodus 31: 16 The people of Isra'el are to keep the Shabbat, to observe Shabbat* **through all their generations** *as a perpetual covenant. 17 It is a sign between me and the people of Isra'el* **forever***; for in six days ADONAI made heaven* *and earth, but on the seventh day he stopped working and rested.'"*

Please note, the Sabbath is a **sign** of YHWH, His seal which represents His authority as Creator. It is what will separate "us believers" from all those who are atheists or who serve other gods!

Those who have the seal or "Mark of God" (Genesis 4:15, Ezekiel 9:4, Ezekiel 9:6, John 6:27, 2 Corinthians 1:2, Ephesians 1: 13, Ephesians 4:30, 2 Timothy 2:19) are the ones who not only have the testimony of our Messiah, but they are also Torah-observant (Revelation 12:17 and 14:12) as was Yeshua who Himself kept kosher and observed the seventh-day Sabbath and the Biblical feasts, etc.

*Revelation 12:17 – "The dragon was infuriated over the woman and went off to fight the rest of her children, those who obey God's commands **and** bear witness to Yeshua."*

*Revelation 14:12 – "This is when perseverance is needed on the part of God's people, those who observe his commands **and** exercise Yeshua's faithfulness."*

"Yeshua's faithfulness" included the fact that He was completely Torah observant – and He NEVER suggested we could toss Torah out the window after His death! Now, who are those who obey God's commands AND bear witness to Yeshua? Certainly not those who refuse to adhere to Torah! The "commands" refer not just to the Ten Commandments but to ALL of YHWH's commands, without which we would be no better than the "heathens"....

We must always remember that YHWH continuously warned Israel not to follow the Gentile nations and their heathen ways:

*Deuteronomy 18: 9 "When you enter the land ADONAI your God is giving you, you are not to learn how to follow the abominable practices of those nations. 10 There must not be found among you anyone who makes his son or daughter pass through fire, a diviner, a soothsayer, an enchanter, a sorcerer, 11 a spell-caster, a consulter of ghosts or spirits, or a necromancer. 12 For whoever does these things is detestable to ADONAI, and because of these abominations ADONAI your God is driving them out ahead of you. 13 You must be wholehearted with ADONAI your God. 14 For these nations, which you are about to dispossess, listen to soothsayers and diviners; but you, ADONAI your God does not allow you to do this.*

## The "Replacement Theology" excuse...

Using certain misunderstood/misinterpreted verses as "proof" that the Jews were cursed and are no longer God's Chosen, some Christians insist that "the church" has replaced Isra'el and they are therefore not required to adhere to Old Testament teachings. For instance:

*Matthew 27: 25. And answered all the people and said, "Let his blood be upon us and upon our children."*

Does the above mean there is a blood curse upon the Jews? No! First, Exodus 20:4 is being referenced here, which indicates that YHWH visits sins up to the fourth generation. Some of the Sanhedrin were concerned that Yeshua was innocent; they concluded that if he was innocent, a worst case scenario would bring a curse on them lasting four generations. However, if Yeshua was guilty and if the Romans became angry, they feared Israel would be wiped off the face of the earth; hence not only four generations but all future generations would be affected. This idea was also stated by the high priest in John 11:48. This grossly misunderstood (or twisted) verse was fashioned into a "the blood curse" by Christians against the Jewish people.

"Replacement theology" seems to be rampant in some of our modern Christian churches. But, what does the Bible say about this?

Moshe (Moses) told the people of Isra'el:

*Deuteronomy 7: 6 For you are a people set apart as holy for ADONAI your God. ADONAI your God has chosen you out of all the peoples on the face of the earth to be his own unique treasure. 7 ADONAI didn't set his heart on you or choose you because you numbered more than any other people - on the contrary, you were the fewest of all peoples. 8 Rather, it was because ADONAI loved you, and because he wanted to keep the oath which he had sworn to your ancestors, that ADONAI brought you out with a strong hand and redeemed you from a life of slavery under the hand of Pharaoh king of Egypt.*

The prophet Jeremiah wrote:

*Jeremiah 31: 36 This is what ADONAI says: "If the sky above can be measured and the foundations of the earth be fathomed, then I will reject all the offspring is Isra'el for all that they have done," says ADONAI.*

And from the prophet Isaiah:

*Isaiah 66: 22 For just as the new heavens and the new earth that I am making will continue in my presence," says ADONAI, "so will your descendants and your name continue. 23 "Every month on Rosh-Hodesh (new moon) and every week on Shabbat, everyone living will come to worship in my presence," says ADONAI.*

In other words, **no one** has replaced the Jews as YHWH's "chosen" and God never changed His "forever" commands to fit into the theology of today's modern Christians. Christians, for the most part, have taken the God of Abraham, Isaac and Jacob, and turned Him into someone unrecognizable. In many cases, He's depicted as a blue-eyed, long-haired, blond "Adonis" instead of the tallit wearing, Sabbath-keeping, Torah observant Jew that He was.

In the allegory of the Olive Tree in Romans 11, Rav Sha'ul (the Apostle Paul) said that the root of the Olive Tree (Isra'el) was holy and that the Gentiles, through the atoning death of Messiah Yeshua, were grafted in and could therefore partake of the nourishing sap from the olive root. He also warned that they shouldn't feel superior because they were not the original holy root; rather, they were "grafted in" branches which could be cut off just as easily as the natural branches.

Being "grafted in" does not in any way mean Christians have "replaced" the Jewish people! There are no "Christian denominations" in YHWH's Kingdom; there is only Isra'el! The grafting in is a great privilege which requires you to realize you are set apart for God (Romans 12:1). And along with the privilege comes the responsibility of obeying His "forever" commands....

*Deuteronomy 5: 26 Oh, how I wish their hearts would stay like this always, that they would fear me and obey all my mitzvot (words/commands); so that it would go well with them and their children forever.*

*Ezekiel 20: 11 I gave them my laws and showed them my rulings; if a person obeys them, he will have life through them. 12 I gave them My Shabbats (Sabbaths) as a sign between me and them, so that they would know that I, ADONAI, am the one who makes them holy.*

# Should Christians be Torah Observant?

# Chapter 4

## Torah was around in "the beginning"....

Returning to our discussion of Torah – Torah goes all the way back to the Garden of Eden when YHWH gave Adam and Eve one simple command, which was to stay away from the Tree of the Knowledge of Good and Evil:

*Genesis 2: 16 ADONAI, God, gave the person this order: "You may eat freely from every tree in the garden 17 except the tree of the knowledge of good and evil. You are not to eat from it, because on the day that you eat from it, it will become certain that you will die."*

YHWH couldn't have made it any clearer: With one exception, Adam and Eve were allowed to eat from every tree in the Garden, including from the "tree of life" (Genesis 2:9). Eating the fruit of the tree of the knowledge of good and evil, however, meant death (note God didn't say "immediate physical death," but "certain" death). Had Adam and Eve chosen to obey God instead of allowing themselves to be deceived by

Satan, things would surely have turned out differently for mankind!

Regardless, here we have the first indication that breaking YHWH's Torah commands is a lethal act – an act that requires an animal sacrifice. Please note that, in Genesis 3:21 we have the earliest animal sin sacrifice because the first thing ADONAI did immediately after confronting Adam and Eve about their transgression was to cover them with the skin of an innocent animal, killed just for them – an animal they had surely known and named!

Shortly after their eviction from the Garden of Eden for disobedience, we are shown the struggles of mankind, beginning with the story of how Cain killed Abel in a jealous rage concerning their sin sacrifice offerings:

*Genesis 4: 2 In addition she (Havah/Eve) gave birth to his brother Hevel (Abel). Hevel kept sheep, while Kayin (Cain) worked the soil. 3 In the course of time Kayin brought an offering to ADONAI from the produce of the soil; 4 and Hevel too brought from the firstborn of his sheep, including their fat. ADONAI accepted Hevel and his offering 5 but did not accept Kayin and his offering. Kayin was very angry and his face fell. 6 ADONAI said to Kayin, "Why are you so angry? Why so downcast? 7 If you are doing what is good, shouldn't you hold your head high? And if you don't do what is good, sin is crouching at the door – it wants you, but you can rule over it."*

At this point, one might question: How did Cain and Abel know they were to give sin offerings to YHWH? Why did the Creator accept Abel's offering and not

Cain's? Did He make up new rules on the spur of the moment? No! The above is evidence that Cain and Abel already knew "right from wrong"; and they knew the rules about sin sacrifices. The whole scenario is proof that Torah - God's teaching and instruction - was clearly around since the beginning!

*Hebrews 9: 22 In fact, according to the Torah, almost everything is purified with blood; indeed, without the shedding of blood there is no forgiveness of sins.*

Although the Bible doesn't tell us exactly where and how YHWH showed His creation the proper way to offer sin sacrifices, the fact remains that the command was passed down at some point; and it continued from one generation to the next - until the day our Savior was crucified; thus, forever abolishing the need for sin sacrifices.

It is imperative, however, to remember that our relationship with God did not end just because Man was prone to sin. Man ultimately suffered the consequences of disobedience - a death sentence - which changed the relationship with YHWH but did not put an end to it, thanks to His patience and mercy.

### Noah knew Torah....

Romans 6:23 tells us, the ultimate consequence of sin is death. In Noah's time, the whole Earth was wiped out because there was a complete rejection of Torah and evil reigned. The flood served as the ultimate warning to mankind that, although our Creator was patient and merciful, He would NOT condone willful sinning.

As we journey through the Tanakh ("Old Testament"), we see that YHWH offered His creation chance after chance to get themselves "right" with Him, but man kept failing. During the time of the flood, only Noah and his family were saved because Noah was "righteous" (Genesis 7:1). During this time YHWH kept escalating His teachings as evidenced in Genesis 9:1-17 which outlines the new covenant He made with Noah and his sons; and from this we can also see that the Earth's steady population growth necessitated more rules and regulations to keep the people in check.

Before we go on, have you ever noticed that in Genesis 7:2-15 God told Noah to take both "clean" and "unclean" animals onto the ark, and that Noah offered only "clean" birds and animals on the altar after he left the ark (Genesis 8:20)? The difference between "clean and unclean" was not actually clarified until the time of the Exodus, but at least we can see that the idea of kosher eating and "proper" sacrifices was already around well before Moses, as we saw in the case of the sacrifices presented by Cain and Abel.

Genesis 9 goes on to tell us that the whole Earth was populated by the three sons of Noah: Shem, Ham and Japheth. It is important to note here, that **neither Noah nor his sons were Hebrew or Jewish!** Neither were Cain and Abel or even Adam and Eve – but yet they were ALL Torah observant! (The term "Hebrew" was first associated with Abram and his sons [beginning in Genesis 12], whom YHWH identified as "Hebrews," chosen to make known His mighty Name and to ultimately bring salvation to the world.)

We have seen that from Adam's time on, man has known about YHWH's demand for obedience, the need for blood sacrifices to atone for sin and about "clean" and "unclean" animals; and, consequently, Christian church leaders have no leg to stand on when they insist that believing Gentiles don't need to be Torah observant because "those old rules applied only to the Jews"…

## Abraham, Isaac and Jacob knew Torah….

As the Bible shows, YHWH continuously revealed Himself to Man, always precisely outlining His divine desires. He never forced new or irrational ideas on Man; rather, He expanded on the **same principles** that ultimately comprised the Ten Commandments (Exodus 34:28) which were presented to Moshe (Moses). Let's briefly discuss what happened on Mt. Sinai:

*Exodus 19: 3 Moshe went up to God, and ADONAI called to him from the mountain: "Here is what you are to say to the household of Ya'akov, to tell the* **people of Isra'el***: 4 'You have seen what I did to the Egyptians, and how I carried you on eagles' wings and brought you to myself. 5 Now if you will pay careful attention to what I say and keep my covenant, then you will be my own treasure from among all the peoples,* *for all the earth is mine; 6 and you will be a kingdom of cohanim (priests) for me, a nation set apart.' These are the words you are to speak to the people of Isra'el."*

Exodus goes on (verses 19:8 and 24:3) to reveal that Isra'el accepted YHWH's offer, which formed the beginning of the Mosaic covenant: *Moshe came and told the people everything ADONAI had said, including all the rulings. The people answered with one voice: "We will obey every word ADONAI has spoken."*

Did you notice that **Isra'el** accepted YHWH's offer and agreed to obey "every word"? Isra'el consisted of "a mixed multitude" who accompanied Moshe out of Egypt (Exodus 12:38). It cannot be reiterated enough that Isra'el includes not only the Hebrews/Jews but anyone who accepts the God of Abraham, Isaac and Jacob (Exodus 12:49 and Numbers 9:14) who is the "same yesterday, today and forever" (Hebrews 13:8). One God, one set of rules! We're all equal in His eyes.

Keeping in mind what you've learned thus far, the question begs to be asked again: Does it make any sense at all that Yeshua would have "nailed" the entire Torah - God's original teachings - to the cross"?

## Divine Law and the priesthood

As we've seen, Divine Law and priesthood have always been around, as far back as Adam and Eve. Once Man had partaken from tree of the knowledge of good and evil, he and his offspring were destined to reap the consequences; and these consequences required sacrifices and offerings to God....

The sacrifice for sin was always the shedding of innocent blood. Why blood? Because blood is our life force; without it, we die. Why an innocent animal? To make man feel the anguish over the loss of an innocent life on his behalf! Something had to die so that we sinners could continue living in God's Presence!

While Adam's children were busy procreating and populating the Earth a high priest was not yet required to perform the sacrifices and so, in those days, every man offered his own sacrifice and acted as his own priest (as in the cases of Abel, Noah, Melchizedek, Job and Abraham).

The need for a high priest – an intercessor between God and man – arose when Isra'el's population began to grow. The priesthood was made up of one High Priest along with many other "regular" priests. The High Priest represented Isra'el as a whole nation before YHWH, while the "regular" priests represented individual Israelites. (Duties of the high priest are outlined in the books of Exodus and Leviticus, in places such as Exodus 28:6-42; 29: 6; 39: 27-29; and Leviticus 6: 19-23 and 21: 10.)

Yeshua haMashiach, YHWH Incarnate, who came to Earth in the form of a Man, ultimately became our High Priest. Yeshua chose to offer Himself on our behalf and bore the sins of all of us permanently – and the only thing required of us, in return, was to "believe" in His shed blood at the cross as our Final Sin Sacrifice, which allowed us to become "new creatures in Christ" who desire to follow **all** God's commandments (Hebrews 3:1; John 3:15-18; 1 Peter 1:18-19; John 10:8-9; John 10:10; 2 Cor. 5:17-18; Matthew 1:21; Isaiah 7:14).

Ultimately, as you know, YHWH made **us** priests to stand and minister in His Name (I Peter 2:5, 2:9, Revelation 1:6, 5:9-10)! But, we can only do this if we are willing to follow ALL of His "forever" commands! YHWH never changed His mind about obedience to Torah or about the punishment for the consequences of sin!

What you've read so far has broadly outlined the history of God's people before the actual giving of the Torah through Moses, which showed that Man always had a relationship with God. YHWH's goal wasn't to impose a myriad hard-to-follow rules on us! His desire for us was to have a blueprint for moral, Godly living which would allow us to continue having a relationship with Him.

(By the way, examples of YHWH's commandments are sprinkled throughout the Torah in places such as Genesis 26:2-5; Exodus 15:25-27; 16; 20:6; Leviticus 22, 26, 27; Numbers 15, 36; Deuteronomy 4, 5, 6, 7, 8, 10, 11, 13, 26, 27, 28, 30, 31. There are more, but you get the picture: God was very adamant about people following **all** His teachings because they were for our own good.)

We also need to remember that, just because Moses was the first one to present God's teachings as "Torah," YHWH – not Moses – is the Creator of the Torah. YHWH shared some of His wisdom with Moses, who was to pass it on to the Hebrews and to those who chose to follow the God of Abraham, Isaac and Jacob.

Are you beginning to see why YHWH said His Torah would stand forever (2 Chronicles 7:14-22)? How could something that is so good for us, ever be considered a "curse" as the Christian church keeps insisting?

As you know, in our fallen state, it is impossible to please God. Unless we have placed our faith and trust in Messiah Yeshua, our Final Sin Sacrifice, we have no other way to obtain eternal life. However, that does not make Torah the "curse of the law"– rather, "the curse" is our endeavor to acquire salvation by following the law without faith because, as mere human beings with limited human mindsets, we are prone to stumble at some point:

*James 2: 8 If you truly attain the goal of Kingdom Torah, in conformity with the passage that says, "Love your neighbor as yourself," you are doing well. 9 But if you show favoritism, your actions constitute sin, since you are convicted under the Torah as transgressors. 10 For a person who keeps the whole Torah, yet stumbles at one point, has become guilty of breaking them all. 11 For the One who said, "Don't commit adultery," also said, "Don't murder." Now, if you don't commit adultery but do murder, you have become a transgressor of the Torah. 12 Keep speaking and acting like people who will be judged by a Torah which gives freedom. 13 For judgment will be without mercy toward one who doesn't show mercy; but mercy wins out over judgment.*

What will the people be judged by (verse 12)? **Torah!** HaShem wasn't "cursing" man when He gave us some guidelines to live by. ALL of His commandments were given for a reason. ALL of His commandments taught man right from wrong, and how to obey God and to worship Him properly. Mashiyach (Messiah) redeemed us from the "curse of the Torah,"[2] by becoming accursed.[3]

It's time the world became aware of the fact that YHWH handed down many more requirements besides just the Ten Commandments, and that He never, ever said to disregard His Torah. Yeshua came to establish and confirm Torah, and also to expose the man-made opinions and traditions that had become

---

2  The "Curse of the Torah" is found in Deuteronomy 27:15-26. There are 12 specific curses mentioned; however, one can also apply this to the entire Torah.  If anyone knowingly or unknowingly sins, but does not seek forgiveness and restitution, they are under the curse. There is a "Y" in the road of every choice we make: one road leads to blessing, the other to a curse.

3  Yeshua was "accursed" by his accusers, but Christians who insist on following man's opinions instead of God's Word, sadly teach that YHWH and Torah accused Yeshua. However, Yeshua was the Perfect Lamb who never broke Torah; therefore, could never come under any curse of Torah. We come under the curse when we sin and refuse to turn to YHWH! (Both footnotes were borrowed from the Netzari Aramaic English Interlinear by Andrew Gabriel Roth).

entangled in God's teachings.  Paul verified this when he said: *Does it follow that we abolish Torah by this trusting? Heaven forbid! On the contrary, we confirm Torah* (Romans 3:31).

Should Christians be Torah Observant?

# Chapter 5

## The misunderstood, misinterpreted writings of Paul

Yeshua attempted to make people realize that He had not come to abolish Torah but, rather, the man-made traditions and the teachings of some of the rabbis who had twisted the Words of ADONAI. But, as has always been the case, Man wasn't listening then, and he isn't listening now because we are **still** misinterpreting the Word of God! Example:

*Matthew 26: 34 Y'shua said to him, Truly I say to you, that in this night before the cock crows you will deny me three times. (Netzari Aramaic English Interlinear)*

Many, if not most pastors have interpreted this to mean a literal rooster. I once listened to a whole sermon where the pastor spoke about how "the rooster" was the only one who was doing God's will that morning. Had this pastor been familiar with Hebrew, he would have been surprised to discover that this passage referred to the "temple crier" – a *Gaver*, Hebrew for "cock" or "rooster," a person responsible for opening the temple before dawn and calling out loudly two or three times to announce the early morning services....

This type of misinterpretation is also true for the much-misunderstood teachings of Rav Sha'ul (Apostle Paul) whose teachings are constantly used by Christians to prove that "the law is a curse and it was nailed to the cross." To wit:

*Colossians 2: 14 He (Yeshua) wiped away the bill of charges against us. Because of the regulations, it stood as a testimony against us; but he removed it by nailing it to the execution-stake. 15 Stripping the rulers and authorities of their power, he made a public spectacle of them, triumphing over them by means of the stake.*

Please note Yeshua wiped away the BILL OF CHARGES (sins) against us, not Torah! Verse 15 goes on to explain what Yeshua nailed to the cross was NOT Torah but rather the man-made laws! The same person who wrote that the Torah is holy just and good could not possibly be referring to the **Torah** as the "certificate of debt" or "bill of charges"! Let's study this a little further:

Referring once more to author and Aramaic scholar Andrew Gabriel Roth, none of the words that mean "Torah" appear in either the Greek or the Aramaic version of Colossians 2:14. This means "Torah" is not meant, because "Torah" never appears! Roth writes:

> "So what then is 'the certificate of debt'? In the original texts the Aramaic word *khawbayn*

means both 'debt' and 'sin'. In addition, Y'shua used the same word in the Sermon on the Mount when he says, *'Forgive our debts/offenses, as we forgive those who are in debt to us/have offended us.'* Interesting to note, half the Greek texts read 'debt' and the other half 'offense' because each group chose one of this word's two meanings.

"However, in Aramaic thought, to be in sin is literally to be in debt! Note also that *khawbayn* is in the plural state, meaning 'the certificate of our debts', as in humanity collectively. That is why Y'shua says elsewhere:

*"Y'shua said to them, 'If you were blind you would have no sin, but since you say 'we see', your sin/debt (Nybwx) remains.*

"And so, the certificate of our debts is simply a record of all the transgressions that we have generated throughout our lives. The Torah tells us what those sins are, but what Y'shua did was to take the transcript of those sins and nail those to the cross! This act of mercy then leaves us in the same position as the adulteress in John 8, who was pardoned by Y'shua – not because she was innocent, but because her accusers had fled. Then Y'shua, who knew she was guilty, could have judged her as the Son of Man, but he let her go because he followed the Torah principle that demanded two witnesses establish her guilt

(Deuteronomy 17:6, 19:15). We notice also that she does not exactly get a free pass to do whatever she pleases because Y'shua adds, 'Go now, and sin no more.'

"So when we are guilty of sin, YHWH is one witness to that guilt, and the record that is generated of that sin is another. However, with the reconcilement of Y'shua on the cross dying in our place, that second witness/record against us is obliterated, and the Torah remains simply to guide us in the path of righteousness for the rest of our redeemed lives."

As you can see, it is very important to know what the original texts state....

At this point it must be mentioned that people today are viewing Paul's writings through a "Greek" as opposed to a Hebrew mindset. If his teachings were being viewed as he had intended, there would be a lot less confusion. After all, why would any God-fearing, obedient believer desire to perpetuate the idea that YHWH would allow Yeshua to nail to the cross the **only** divine blueprint for moral behavior? What possessed us to think we could **dare** view His original teachings as a "curse"?

We need to give Paul, the emissary to the Gentiles, some credit because, unless one is bilingual or has studied a foreign language, they will find it hard to fathom the frustration he must have experienced in trying to convey the complicated messages of the Hebrew language into Greek....

Be that as it may, a thorough study of Paul's writings read in context reveals that he **never** went against Yeshua's teachings, nor did he ever renounce the Torah – although many Christians like to cite text from places such as Galatians 2:3-16 as "proof" that he did. Unless one is viewing Paul's writings through a "Hebrew mindset," these verses seem to show that he suggests Gentiles don't need to be circumcised; but nothing could be further from the truth, as explained in a footnote on Galatians 2 in Roth's Netzari Aramaic English Interlinear:

> Unlike the contemporary traditions of Judaism in Paul's day, a soul who follows Mashiyach is not immediately forced to be circumcised once they show interest, as this is something that is done according to the intent of a person's heart. Circumcision is a voluntary choice, just as it would also be unthinkable to force someone to be immersed (baptized). Every soul must willfully volunteer to fulfill their obligations as their soul is being matured by the Ruach haKodesh. Paul clearly indicates that the requirement for circumcision has in NO way been negated. Circumcision is a demonstration of Faith and Obedience when a person does so according to the leading of the Ruach haKodesh (Holy Spirit), but NOT

on the basis of social, peer, or status quo pressure.

Furthermore, a comparison between Galatians 2 and Romans 2:13-14 reveals that Paul, in fact, is NOT speaking against the Torah at all:

*Romans 2: 13 For it is not merely the hearers of the Torah whom God considers righteous; rather, it is the doers of what Torah says who will be made righteous in God's sight. 14 For whenever Gentiles, who have no Torah, do naturally what the Torah requires, then these, even though they don't have Torah, for themselves are Torah!*

Again, footnotes from Roth's Netzari Aramaic English Interlinear explain:

> (Ref. Romans 2:13) Notice how those "under Torah" and those "doers of Torah" are put in opposition to one another; therefore, both cannot simultaneously be in error. This is clarified with the phrase "for doers of Torah will be made righteous." So, if Torah-doers are made righteous, it stands to reason Torah itself is NOT passing away! The fact that such deep pro-Torah statements are being sent to Gentiles in Rome speaks volumes of how mainstream Christianity is perverting Rav Shaul's teachings. "Under Torah" means to look to its rituals as a form of magic; a power that needs no purity of intent to bring about blessing, but merely fixed repetition. Torah in itself provides no authority of magic rather, Torah has authority because it is

YHWH's instruction to man! So "under Torah" is a false teaching that has never been true according to the Tanakh ("Old Testament"): YHWH blesses man for Torah observance, which is obedience to His Commandments. Notice in Matthew 15 how Y'shua rebukes the Pharisees on this very issue, how they set aside YHWH's Torah (instructions) in favor of their traditions.

(Ref. Romans 2:14) Rav Shaul does not suggest that Gentiles are spontaneously mastering Torah. The point is they should learn the written Torah without distraction from Pharisaic traditions which are not rooted in the plain understanding of Torah.

Moving on, Acts 21:15-21, which was written after Paul wrote the Galatians, clearly reveals that he was Torah observant, and that his teachings (especially the misconception in Romans 8 that, "if someone is led by the Spirit, they are not under law..." and Galatians 3 that "the law is a curse") have been severely misunderstood because Paul was referring not to Torah but to **man's** law/legalism.

Many Christians insist there is nothing in the New Covenant that commands us to be Torah observant, or which suggests we continue to adhere to any of the commands of the "Old Testament." But, if that were the case, then how would they explain Romans 3:31?

And what about this next scripture?

73

*Colossians 2:16 - So don't let anyone pass judgment on you in connection with eating and drinking, or in regard to a Jewish festival or Rosh-Hodesh or Shabbat.*

Was Paul negating Torah, or in any way suggesting that being kosher, or keeping any of the festivals or the seventh day Sabbath was now taboo? No! He was warning about the **opinions of men** concerning these things – He was not giving permission to ignore the rules!

*Romans 14: 5 One person considers some days more holy than others, while someone else regards them as being all alike. What is important is for each to be fully convinced in his own mind. 6 He who observes a day as special does so to honor the Lord. Also he who eats anything, eats to honor the Lord, since he gives thanks to God; likewise the abstainer abstains to honor the Lord, and he too gives thanks to God.*

Does the above suggest that Paul said it is up to each of us to decide what we should eat and what day we should keep?

Absolutely not! The context of this passage was a dispute over whether one can eat food that may or may not have been offered to idols. In those days food that may or may not have been offered to idols was usually put out for sale to people on a certain day of the week – and some believers refused to purchase or eat food on those days, just to be on the safe side. On the other hand, some did because they figured, since they didn't know for sure whether or not it had been offered, it wouldn't be wrong to eat it.

In the previous Scripture (Romans 14:5-6) Paul was not addressing kosher foods or Sabbath day observance at all; he was referring to the disagreement over whether market place food, because of idolatry, should be bought and eaten on a certain day of the week.

Please check out David H. Stern's explanation in the preface of his Complete Jewish Bible, wherein he demonstrates the difference between "kosher" and "ceremonially clean." Stern says YHWH **never** said pork, shellfish, etc. were food. People called these animals food in rebellion against God....

The passages in Romans are dealing with animals YHWH gave us to eat and whether they are ceremonially clean and can be eaten at that time. Even in Peter's vision (Acts 11), Peter would never have eaten the kosher animals that had been in contact with *treif* (non-kosher) animals. The vision was to show that, as Peter knew which animals were clean and which were not because as God had shown him, Peter was to accept the Gentiles as God had now shown him they were "clean". The rest of the passage in Acts 11 shows that this is the correct interpretation and what the vision was all about (see Acts 11:18).

Now, consider the following passage from the book of Hebrews which many Christians attempt to use to show that the Old Covenant of Moses (which was all about Torah!) was completely replaced:

*Hebrews 10: 8 In saying first, "You neither willed nor were pleased with animal sacrifices, meal offerings, burnt offerings*

75

*and sin offerings," things which are offered in accordance with the Torah; 9 and then, "Look, I have come to do your will"; he takes away the first system in order to set up the second.*

Does the above recommend **abolition** of the Mosaic Covenant? No! Since we know that YHWH and not Moses was the author of Torah, and that Torah dates all the way back to Adam and Eve, when read in context, we can see that through Yeshua the covenant wasn't abolished but merely transformed/ revised/clarified/updated to meet God's needs for the sake of the next generation of Earth's population explosion!

Hebrews 2:17 explains what Hebrews 10:8-9 is all about:

*Hebrews 2:17 This is why He had to become like his brothers in every respect – so that He might become a merciful and faithful cohen gadol (high priest) in the service of God, making kapparah (atonement) for the sins of the people.*

YHWH no longer required sin sacrifices, thanks to the New Covenant Sin sacrifice of Yeshua. In Hebrews 2:17 Paul attempts to explain that the animal sin sacrifice does not take away sins, but that Yeshua's sacrifice renders useless any other offering for sin. Then, in Hebrews 5:13-6:1 He relates the importance of the Messiah to the maturing of intellect.

Nowhere in Hebrews or anywhere else, for that matter, does Paul ever claim that Torah has been abolished! On the contrary, he explains that those who disobey Torah remain guilty, and that if they ignore the shed blood of Yeshua they will face severe judgment. Furthermore, Paul, throughout Hebrews 10, refers to being "made holy"– explaining that holiness isn't obtained just by believing in Messiah but by observing Torah (see Numbers 15:40 and Proverbs 4:2).

Now, let's examine Ephesians 2:15-16 to see whether it implies that Yeshua abolished Torah:

*Ephesians 2:15 by destroying in his own body the enmity occasioned by the Torah, with its commands set forth in the form of ordinances. He did this in order to create in union with himself from the two groups a single new humanity and thus make shalom, 16 and in order to reconcile to God both in a single body by being executed on a stake as a criminal and thus killing in himself that enmity.*

Again, there's nothing to imply that Torah was negated. When Yeshua was physically present on Earth, He attempted to show how senseless was the animosity between the two groups caused by the opinions of men concerning Torah. Through Him, "one new man" was made from the two separate groups.

*Colossians 2: 20 If, along with the Messiah, you died to the elemental spirits of the world, then why, as if you still belonged to the world, are you letting yourselves be bothered by its rules? - 21 "Don't touch this!" "Don't eat that!" "Don't handle the other!"*

In the above, did Paul say we are to ignore the Old Testament commandments today? No - absolutely not! He's again talking about the opinions of men, not about YHWH's Word which has always been holy and good!

In Colossians 2:23, Paul attempted to thwart the creation of more human opinions by writing:

*They do indeed have the outward appearance of wisdom, with their self-imposed religious observances, false humility and asceticism; but they have no value at all in restraining people from indulging their old nature.*

Many Christians argue that Paul said we could eat whatever we want, meaning there is no more kashrut/kosher (the set of dietary laws governing what can or cannot be eaten). Please read the following passage very carefully:

*1 Timothy 4: 1 The Spirit expressly states that in the acharit-hayamim (coming age) some people will apostatize from the faith by paying attention to deceiving spirits and things taught by demons. 2 Such teachings come from the hypocrisy of liars whose own consciences have been burned, as if with a red-hot branding iron. 3 They forbid marriage and require abstinence from foods which God created to be eaten with thanksgiving by those who have come to trust and to know the truth. 4 For everything created by God is good, and nothing received with thanksgiving needs to be rejected, 5 because the word of God and prayer make it holy.*

Christians have interpreted verse 4 as all foods being declared "good". This is quite wrong! First, we have to remember that Paul was talking to the Jews who ate only kosher foods. They wouldn't dream of going against what YHWH said in Leviticus about what He considered to be food. Kosher Law is still God's Law, and Paul actually confirmed that fact. In 1 Timothy 4, he warned against "doctrines of demons" which say one can't have certain foods which God has said are good to eat. Paul is saying every clean creature is good and not to be refused **if** it is made holy by the Word of God and prayer (thanksgiving). It is understood which foods are "clean" and which are not. Leviticus tells us what is holy and not holy. The word kosher comes from the same root as *kodesh,* meaning holy.

The books of Leviticus and Deuteronomy specify what can and cannot be consumed. According to YHWH's Torah, the animals considered "clean" have cloven hooves and ruminate (chew their cud). Swine are considered to be unclean because, while their hooves are cloven, they don't chew their cud. Paul knew this; he did not negate or change it. (And if he HAD EVER attempted to show that any part of Torah had been negated or abolished, we would have to ask ourselves: Who are we to believe – Yeshua, God Incarnate who was completely Torah observant, or the MAN, Paul? If Paul had truly been anti-Torah as the Church suggests, then surely YHWH wouldn't have allowed the writings of Paul to be included in the Bible!)

Although it may not make sense to our limited human mindsets, YHWH had His reasons for kashrut laws, and if you don't have access to a computer, it would behoove you to buy a good book on this subject because it's extremely important.

## Getting back to YHWH's Torah:

It cannot be over-emphasized that Yeshua abolished the need for sin sacrifices and that He came to abolish the "rabbinical" teachings of the time that had people so bound up in "legalism" that they were afraid to get out of bed on the Sabbath for fear of being guilty of "working." The teachings of the rabbis of old had made the entire Torah a burden. Acts 21:20-24 tells us:

*Acts 21: 20 On hearing it, they praised God; but they also said to him, "You see, brother, how many tens of thousands of believers there are among the Judeans, and they are all zealots for the Torah. 21 Now what they have been told about you is that you are teaching all the Jews living among the Goyim to apostatize from Moshe, telling them not to have a b'rit-milah (circumcision) for their sons and not to follow the traditions. 22 What, then, is to be done? They will certainly hear that you have come. 23 So do what we tell you. We have four men who are under a vow. 24 Take them with you, be purified with them, and pay the expenses connected with having their heads shaved. Then everyone will know that there is nothing to these rumors which they have heard about you: but that, on the contrary, you yourself stay in line and keep the Torah.*

Let's ask ourselves this: If Yeshua had indeed abolished the "law," then why did the apostle Paul observe it with four other church men in Yerushalayim (Jerusalem) 29 years **after** the crucifixion of Messiah (Acts 21:23-24)? Paul wrote:

*Romans 7: 7 Therefore, what are we to say? That the Torah is sinful? Heaven forbid!* **Rather, the function of the Torah was that without it, I would not have known what sin is.** *For example, I would not have become conscious of what greed is if the Torah had not said, "Thou shalt not covet."*

*Romans 7: 12* **So the Torah is holy;** *that is, the commandment is holy, just and good.*

Paul also said that YHWH's law is spiritual (Romans 7:14) - and that which is spiritual is eternal.

*2 Corinthians 4: 18 We concentrate not on what is seen but on what is not seen, since things seen are temporary, but things not seen are eternal.*

So, the question once more is: Why would Yeshua's death have abolished Torah? Those who teach contrary to the Torah, which both Yeshua and Paul upheld, are false preachers and prophets; nothing more, nothing less. Paul wrote:

*2 Corinthians 11: 13 The fact is that such men are pseudo-emissaries: they tell lies about their work and masquerade as emissaries of the Messiah. 14 There is nothing surprising in that, for the Adversary himself masquerades as an angel of light; 15 so it's no great thing if his workers masquerade as servants of righteousness. They will meet the end their deeds deserve.*

Again – is Torah still valid today? You bet it is! It is our standard for righteousness. Yeshua said that not one yud (smallest letter in the Hebrew alphabet) or tittle (a small distinctive mark such as a diacritic/accent or the dot over an i or a j) would pass away, and that those who love Him will keep His commandments. Torah is not for salvation, but for sanctification (being Holy).

Regardless as to how much the Christian world struggles to prove otherwise, the fact is, **Paul taught the Kingdom of Elohim**, testifying of Messiah Yeshua and the Book of the Torah. As Acts 28:23 clearly shows, Paul taught *"out of the Torah of Moshe, and out of the prophets,"* from morning till evening. He gave a very stern warning when he said:

Hebrews 10:28-29: *"For if he who transgressed the Torah of Moshe, died without mercies at the mouth of two or three witnesses; how much more, do you think, will he receive capital punishment who has trodden upon the Son of Elohim and has accounted the blood of his covenant by which he is sanctified, as the blood of all men and has treated the Spirit of grace in an insulting manner?"* (Netzari Aramaic English Interlinear).

By comparing YHWH's capital punishment from the Torah of Moshe with violations against the "blood of his covenant" or against the "Spirit of grace" Paul clearly taught that Torah is a Living Covenant that was never abolished!

No one can keep the Torah perfectly (but thanks to Yeshua we are forgiven!); however, striving to live as ELOHIM commands brings us closer to His desire for our lives.

# Chapter 6

## What parts of Torah can we still observe today?

If we're talking about all of ADONAI's various commands and "do's" and "don'ts" in general, the logical answer is: We need to observe whatever we possibly can, to the best of our abilities.

Many people believe Torah consists only of "those old 613 commandments." While YHWH did hand down the Commandments, He never numbered them. The 613 *Mitzvot* (Commandments) were more of a man-made tradition rather than an actual list of numbered commandments.

The idea originated in the Talmud ("Oral Torah" which consists of the ideas of the ancient rabbis who were desperately trying to understand the Word of YHWH) which says there are both "positive" and "negative" *mitzvot* (do's and don'ts) which can be divided into 365 Negative *Mitzvot* (which we are told remind us every day of the year to keep us from doing bad things) plus 248 Positive *Mitzvot* (coincidentally the number of bones in the human body) for a total of 613.

Correspondingly, the *tzitzit* (knotted fringes) of the *tallit* (prayer shawl) are also connected to the 613 commandments. Torah commentator Rashi suggested that the number of knots on a *tzitzit* (in its Mishnaic spelling) has the value of 600. When doubled over, each tassel has eight threads and five sets of knots, which totals 13 – for a grand total of 613 – thus, wearers of a *tallit* are reminded of all Torah commandments.

Of the "613 Commandments" most cannot be kept today because they were prescribed for the priests and kings of the day, while some were only for men and others for women. However, there were some commandments that were meant to last throughout eternity. These include:

- **The Ten Commandments:** (Please see Exodus 20; 31:18; 34:29; Deuteronomy 5:5 which included several "forever" commandments).

- **The Seventh Day Sabbath:** (Genesis 2:3; Exodus 20:8; 31:13; 31:16-17; Leviticus 23:3; Deuteronomy 5:12; Isaiah 66:23 and Isaiah 58:13).

- **The Biblical feasts:** Outlined in Leviticus 23 which states after each feast: *"it shall be a statute for ever in all your dwellings throughout your generations."*

- **Keeping kosher.** Yes, eating "clean" foods was a "forever" command. For a complete outline, see Deuteronomy 14:1-21 and Leviticus 11.

The above is by no means exhaustive, but can be counted among some of the most visible of the *mitzvot*.

Man has always liked to "pick and choose" when it comes to the Bible, but it's time to learn some of those "forever" commands – including the concept of the seventh-day Sabbath and the Biblical feasts which are YHWH's appointed times. Each one is significant in that Yeshua is foreshadowed in them. As a matter of fact, Yeshua has so far only fulfilled the first four of the seven feasts – and the next one should be what Christians are calling the "Rapture." Let's discuss these a little further....

## Why should we keep the Biblical feasts?

The original and eternal Feasts of YHWH are everlasting appointments between YHWH and His People and are clearly prophesied to carry on into the Seventh Millennium and beyond into the world to come.

Isaiah 66:23 *"And it shall come to pass, that from one new moon to another, and from one sabbath to another, shall all flesh come to worship before me, says YHWH."*

YHWH designed His appointed times, the *mo'adim*, for His people to come together to worship Him. The fact that all flesh will one day worship YHWH according to **one** calendar tells us that the *mo'adim* are not for Jews only, but for all the Household of Faith as One Body. ("His people" includes anyone who has been "grafted in" to the Olive Tree [Isra'el] to worship the risen Messiah.)

The Creator appointed seven feasts to be celebrated each year:

- Passover (Pesach)

- Unleavened Bread (Hag HaMatzot)

- Firstfruits (Yom HaBikkurim)

- Fifty days after Firstfruits is the Feast of Weeks (Shavuot)

- Feast of Trumpets (Rosh Hashanah)

- Day of Atonement (Yom Kippur)

- Feast of Tabernacles (Sukkot)

YHWH, who is continuously revealing Himself to us, provided some interesting clues to show the importance of His appointed times! The first three major events for believers in Yeshua (His death, burial and resurrection) happened on the first three feasts, and the presentation of the Holy Spirit (what Christians refer to as Pentecost) came 50 days later:

- While Passover was being celebrated (which included the slaying of an unblemished lamb) our Savior, was being slain on the cross (1 Corinthians 5:7).

- The Feast of Unleavened Bread is a foreshadowing of sanctification as Yeshua was buried. Leaven represents sin and, as you know, Yeshua was sinless.

- Firstfruits, celebrated on the morning after the first Sabbath following the feast of Unleavened Bread (Leviticus 23:10-11), is symbolic of Yeshua being the Firstfruits (1 Corinthians 15:23).

- Shavuot (the Feast of Weeks) celebrates the first-fruits of the wheat harvest and the giving of the Torah. It also commemorates the giving of the Holy Spirit to the gathering of believers in Jerusalem (Acts 2), and it fell on the next feast 50 days later (on what Christians call Pentecost)!

Since Yeshua fulfilled the first four Biblical Feasts, the next event – what Christians refer to as the "Rapture"– should fall on Rosh Hashanah, the Feast of Trumpets, when YHWH will call his people together on a day of re-gathering and rejoicing.

Judging from the "forever" importance that YHWH placed on His Feasts, why would anyone think "Jesus abolished" them?

Some have questioned as to how Yeshua could fulfill any feasts after His death. The answer is simple: Because God is forever; He has no beginning and no end. The fleshly body He sent temporarily to teach us about Himself died, but His Spirit didn't. We know He is alive because He rose and because no body was ever found in the sealed tomb in which He was buried! The Bible tells us that Yeshua was with His Father YHWH at the beginning (John 1:1-2) and that He remains a priest forever (Hebrews 7:3).

## God's timeline

Man tends to view things from a linear viewpoint and timeline, whereas YHWH does not. He's God, so why should He have to fulfill everything within our concept of time? His Biblical feasts were given to us for a reason – in part, so that man could know what all was supposed to happen and what was yet to come; that is also why Yeshua was foreshadowed in each one of them!

If YHWH is the same today, yesterday and tomorrow, why would He suddenly want us to ignore His feasts/appointed times? Does it make sense that, just because Yeshua died, it would automatically negate the other three feasts He has yet to fulfill?

*Proverbs 3: 1 "My son, do not forget my teaching [Torah], but keep my commands in your heart."*

*Proverbs 6: 23 For the mitzvah (word) is a lamp,* **Torah is light***, and reproofs that discipline are the way to life.*

*Psalms 1: 1 How blessed are those who reject the advice of the wicked, don't stand on the way of sinners or sit where scoffers sit! 2* **Their delight is in ADONAI's Torah***; on his Torah they meditate day and night. 3 They are like trees planted by streams – they bear their fruit in season, their leaves never wither, everything they do succeeds.*

*Deuteronomy 6: 4 "Sh'ma, Yisrae'el! ADONAI Eloheinu, ADONAI echad [Hear, Isra'el! ADONAI our God, ADONAI is one; 5 and you are to love ADONAI your God with all your heart, all your being and all your resources. 6 These words, which I am ordering you today, are to be on your heart; 7 and you are to teach them carefully to your children. You are to talk about them when you sit at home, when you are traveling on the road, when you lie down and when you get up. 8 Tie them on your hand as a sign, put them at the front of a headband around your forehead, 9 and write them on the door-frames of your house and on your gates.*

Before we go on, did you notice verse 4 which said, "...Hear, Isra'el..."?  Who is Isra'el again?

### Let's discuss the seventh-day Sabbath....

Keeping the Sabbath, one of the Ten Commandments, was not a suggestion! The Bible promises spiritual blessings for those who keep the Sabbath on the day YHWH set apart as holy.

*Isaiah 56: 1"Observe justice, do what is right, for my salvation is close to coming, my righteousness to being revealed." 2 Happy is the person who does this, anyone who grasps it firmly, who keeps Shabbat and does not profane it, and keeps himself from doing any evil.*

*Isaiah 56: 4 For here is what ADONAI says: "As for the eunuchs who keep my Shabbats, who choose what pleases me and hold fast to my covenant: 5 in my house, within my walls, I will give them power and a name greater than sons and daughters; I will give him an everlasting name that will not be cut off. 6 **And the foreigners** who join themselves to ADONAI to serve him, to love the name of ADONAI and to be his workers, **all who keep Shabbat and do not profane it,** and hold fast to my covenant, 7 I will bring them to my holy mountain and make them joyful in my house of prayer....*

YHWH blessed the seventh day and even observed it, Himself (Genesis 2:2-3). The Word tells us the seventh day of the week is God's holy Sabbath day for as long as heaven and earth shall last (Exodus 20:8-11, Matthew 5:17-19, 1 John 3:4).

*Isaiah 58: 13 If you hold back your foot on Shabbat from pursuing your own interests on my holy day; if you call Shabbat a delight, ADONAI'S holy day, worth honoring; then honor it by not doing your usual things or pursuing your interests or speaking about them. 14 If you do, you will find delight in ADONAI - I will make you ride on the heights of the land and feed you with the heritage of your ancestor Ya'akov, for the mouth of ADONAI has spoken."*

*Isaiah 66: 23 "Every month on Rosh-Hodesh and every week on Shabbat, everyone living will come to worship in my presence," says Adonai.*

Please note that the Prophets strongly condemned Sabbath desecration (Ezekiel 20:19-24; Ezekiel 22:8, 26, 31; and Jeremiah 17:27). Yeshua, Paul and the other disciples also kept the Sabbath holy (Luke 4:16). As a matter of fact, in Matthew 24:20 Yeshua, who was telling His disciples about future events, said: "Pray that you will not have to escape in winter or on Shabbat." Since YHWH commanded the SEVENTH day Sabbath and Yeshua kept the seventh-day Sabbath, He certainly wasn't referring to a SUNDAY Sabbath in the future!

## Most are not keeping the true Sabbath!

As mentioned before, both believing Jews and Gentiles regularly attended the synagogue for worship on the seventh day Sabbath (Acts 13:42-44).

The seventh day Sabbath, which the Bible tells us will continue into the new heavens and the new Earth (Exodus 20:12 and 20, Isaiah 66:22-23), is an eternal covenant and divine Sign from YHWH. It serves as a reminder for us to remember and celebrate His work of creation, sanctification and salvation through His Messiah. Even the "New Testament" gives us the following advice about Sabbath keeping:

*Hebrews 4: 9 So there remains a Shabbat-keeping for God's people. 10 For the one who has entered God's rest has also rested from his own works, as God did from his. 11 Therefore, let us do our best to enter that rest; so that no one will fall short because of the same kind of disobedience.*

Despite scriptural evidence concerning the Sabbath and its importance, many, if not most Christians will argue to the death that the seventh-day Sabbath was abolished at the cross and changed to Sunday because

"Jesus rose on a Sunday." The questions remain, however:

- Did Yeshua really rise on a Sunday?

- And if He did, where's the scripture to support that YHWH ever said His Sabbath is now supposed to be on the first day (Sunday)?

Let's check and see what the Bible shows us about the Resurrection from a "Hebrew perspective" which becomes clear when we allow Scripture to interpret Scripture – and reveals that Yeshua was resurrected toward the end of the Sabbath; not early on a Sunday morning (the first day), as is commonly believed:

*Matthew 12: 39 He replied, "A wicked and adulterous generation asks for a sign? No! None will be given to it but the sign of the prophet Yonah.*

*Matthew 16: 4 A wicked and adulterous generation is asking for a sign? It will certainly not be given a sign – except the sign of Yonah!" With that he left them and went off.*

What was the "sign of Yonah/Jonah"?

*Matthew 12: 40 For just as Yonah was three days and three nights in the belly of the sea-monster, so will the Son of Man be three days and three nights in the depths of the earth. 41 The people of Ninveh will stand up at the Judgment with this generation and condemn it, for they turned from their sins to God when Yonah preached, but what is here now is greater than Yonah.*

The SIGN for which we are searching is "Three days and three nights" (Luke 24:21) from death/burial to resurrection of our Savior.

*Matthew 16: 21 From that time on, Yeshua began making it clear to his talmidim that he had to go to Yerushalayim and endure much suffering at the hands of the elders, the head cohanim and the Torah-teachers; and that he had to be put to death; but that on the third day, he had to be raised to life.*

*Matthew 17: 23 ...who will put him to death, and on the third day he will be raised."....*

*Matthew 20: 19 ...and turn him over to the Goyim, who will jeer at him, beat him and execute him on a stake as a criminal. But on the third day, he will be raised."*

(See also Matthew 27:64; Mark 9:31; Mark 10:34; Luke 9:22; Luke 13:32; Luke 18:33; Luke 24:7; Luke 24:46; Acts 10:40; and 1 Corinthians 15:4.)

A thorough study of the Bible reveals that Yeshua was in the grave three days and three nights, and it tells us that He died on Passover, 14 Nisan, which was during the High Holy Days (Leviticus 23:5).

He was in the grave just before sunset on Wednesday night, according to Scripture (John 19:31); all day Thursday and Thursday night; all day Friday and Friday night, and all day Saturday (as Jonah was in the whale three days and three nights) until just before sunset on Saturday when He was resurrected.

93

To discern exactly when our Savior rose, it is important to recognize a few things – beginning with the fact that the dawning of a new day according to YHWH and the Hebrew calendar is at twilight as it is getting dark; not at first light in the morning:

*Genesis 1: 5 God called the light Day, and the darkness he called Night. So there was evening, and there was morning one day.*

We also need to note the time that Yeshua was placed into the grave, which was just before sunset – or approximately 5 p.m. (March-April timeframe).

### Three days and three nights....

No matter what the days are called on our modern calendars, there is no way that three days and three nights beginning sometime in Wednesday evening can end early on Sunday morning – which is what most Christian scholars are trying to insist.

The Bible tells us that Yeshua died at 3 p.m. (the ninth hour - John 19:14 – the day had only 12 "hours" in this era); that He was buried later that day (John 19:31); and that He was in the grave "three days and three nights."

*Matthew 27: 46 And about the ninth hour, Y'shua cried out with a loud voice and said, My El! My El! Why have you spared me?*[1] (Scripture reference and footnote from Netzari Aramaic English Interlinear; see also Mark 15:33-34 and Luke 23:44)

This being just before the High Holy Day (a "High Sabbath," Nissan 15, not a regular Saturday Sabbath), the Judeans wanted Him off the cross and in the grave before sundown so as not to desecrate the holiday, which meant He was in the grave at

---

4 Y'shua was not necessarily quoting Psalm 22, although the imagery of the Psalm is certainly intended by Matthew. Greek is transliterated Eli, Eli lama sabacthani, but Peshitta and Psalm 22 read: Eli, Eli lama azbatani. Many Bibles read "forsaken" from which came a false teaching that the Father left Y'shua destitute (Marcionite thinking). Isaiah 53:4 indicates that "we" reckoned him smitten of Elohim, but it is not YHWH who tortured his own son; it was men motivated by religious tradition. Psalm 22 references those who scorned Y'shua for his Faith in YHWH, and called him a worm (detested), but Father YHWH does not forsake the righteous, nor does He at any time "forsake" His own Son, see Psalm 9:9, 10; 37:25; 71:11; Isaiah 49:14-16.

Y'shua says "Eli" (my El). He is in great physical pain after being brutally tortured; those around him were confused to what he was saying, "Eli-yah" or "Eliyahu". If Hebrew eyewitnesses were not sure of what he was saying, it shouldn't be a surprise that Greek transliteration was also wrong, putting "lama sabacthani" rather than "lemana shabakthani". Perhaps the reason Y'shua says "why are you sparing me" is because he has proven his commitment by laying down his life and has already endured about 6 hours of the execution! So, it's not a matter of being "forsaken" but that he literally means, "Father, I'm ready, why can't we finish this?" In a matter of moments from saying this, he dies, which fully supports this interpretation.

approximately 5 p.m. by modern time keeping shortly after His crucifixion - which means that three days and three nights later would also fall at approximately 5 p.m. Here are the Scriptures to verify these facts:

*John 19: 14 ... it was about noon on Preparation Day of Pesach (Passover)...*

*John 19: 31 It was Preparation Day, and the Judeans did not want the bodies to remain on the stake on Shabbat, since it was an especially important Shabbat...*

Now, many people think this Shabbat fell on a Friday (since God's seven-day cycle begins at sundown on Friday evening). However, as we mentioned above, John 19:14 tells us this "preparation day" was not for a regular Shabbat, but for a High Holy Shabbat. Therefore, the Judeans wanted the bodies of Yeshua and the thieves off the crosses before sundown on Preparation Day, as the next day, Thursday, was a Sabbath.

This means that Yeshua was placed in his grave before sunset that evening, Wednesday.

*John 19: 41 In the vicinity of where he had been executed was a garden, and in the garden was a new tomb in which no one had ever been buried. 42 So, because it was Preparation Day for the Judeans, and because the tomb was close by, that is where they buried Yeshua.*

The above Scripture shows that Yeshua was placed in the heart of the earth approximately 5:00 p.m., or before sunset on the day He died. Three days and three nights must end at the time we start the counting – about 5:00 p.m., or before sunset, that night.

Even on the eve of His death, Yeshua kept and fulfilled the Passover: He died on Wednesday the 14th of Nisan, and He rose some time after 3:00 p.m. on the Sabbath exactly three days later, depending on when He was placed in the grave.

The Sabbath is in commemoration of YHWH's rest at Creation (Genesis 2:2), and Yeshua's rest after His redemption of mankind. The Sabbath is for a reminder of the **sign** (three days and three nights) of who Yeshua haMashyiach (Messiah) is: He the Lord of the Sabbath.

Now, exactly how do we know that He died on the 14th of Nisan and that particular 14th of Nisan fell on a Wednesday? Because the 14th of Nisan is the day on which YHWH declared that the Feast of Passover should be celebrated **forever** (Leviticus 23; Exodus 12:14)! And because of a series of events that took place just prior to the crucifixion:

- Yeshua, the Passover Lamb, fulfilled Zechariah 9:9 when, on 10 Nisan (a Sabbath - Saturday), He rode into Jerusalem on a donkey, as the people waved palm branches: *9 Rejoice with all your heart, daughter of Tziyon! Shout out loud, daughter of Yerushalayim! Look! Your king is coming to you. He is righteous, and he is victorious. Yet he is humble - he's riding on a donkey, yes, on a lowly donkey's colt.* The Bible tells us that it was a Sabbath Day's journey from Bethany. He then taught in the Temple for three days: Sunday, Monday and Tuesday.

- As promised in Exodus 12:25-28 there was to be an explanation of the Passover service. This Messianic fulfillment took place when Yeshua showed His disciples how to celebrate the Passover Seder the evening before His death. During this time He explained how **He is** the fulfillment of the Passover seder (Luke 22:14-20 and 1 Corinthians 11:23-26). Just as He delivered the Israelites with a mighty hand from the bondage of Egypt, so He delivered us from the bondage of sin! It was here that He explained the meaning of His person in the Passover elements. Afterwards, He and His disciples went to Gethsemane, where they spent part of the night.

- During the night Yeshua was arrested and we are told that His trial continued until approximately 9 a.m., when He was crucified. At 3:00 p.m. (the 9th hour) on Wednesday He died.

But, how do we know He was resurrected before the weekly Sabbath (what we call "Saturday") ended?

Because Yeshua was buried just before sunset on Wednesday, 14 Nisan. Scripture verifies this. This made that evening, after sunset, the first "night." Then at sunrise Thursday, we have the first "day." The second "night" then, was Thursday night, followed by the second "day," Friday morning; the third night Friday evening, and the third "day" Saturday after sunrise. Thus, Yeshua rose during the daylight hours on the Shabbat, upon completing "3 days and 3 nights." Had He not risen till Shabbat was over, after sunset, he would have been in the grave "3 days and 4 nights." Yeshua rose sometime during the Shabbat, when Mary Magdalene and the other Mary were in observance of the Shabbat (Luke 23:56).

*Matthew 28: 1 Now in the closing (evening) of the Sabbath, as the first of the week was dawning, came Maryam of Magdala and the other Maryam that they might see the grave.* (Netzari Aramaic English Interlinear)

Andrew Gabriel Roth in his Netzari Aramaic English Interlinear, says the following:

> Aramaic literally reads *"b'ramsha din b'shabata"*, or "in the evening of the Shabbat". The literal meaning of *ramsha* is "evening" or *erev*, but here it is used idiomatically. The dawn and set of the sun is not the only use; there is the "dawn of a new era" or as John 19:31 reads *"mitil d'shabata negha"*, "the Shabbat was dawning." When we compare other verses that record this event, the time of the day being referred

to is clearly more than half a day before literal dawn. In John chapter 19, when they put Y'shua into the tomb, they still refer to it as being "day", both in Aramaic and Greek. The "dawn" metaphor "to begin" is confirmed in John 19:42. A more literal form, *"mitil d'shabata aiala"*, would be read as "the Sabbath was beginning/ entering/ coming about". What is true for "dawning" is also true of "setting" in the sense of "conclusion", as is meant here. This agrees with Greek version, Aramaic information in Matthew, and with other writers in the NT.

The bottom line is that, by the time the two Marys arrived at Yeshua's tomb, Yeshua was nowhere to be found because He was already gone! Since He died at the ninth hour [3 p.m.], three days and three nights later would make it 3 p.m. on Saturday....

As shown above, the Scriptures – read in context – are abundantly clear as to when our Savior died, when He was buried, and when He was resurrected. He did not rise on Sunday. Even if He HAD, the Bible nowhere tells us that we were allowed to change YHWH's seventh day Sabbath to the first day of the week, regardless as to the exact time of His resurrection. Therefore, there is absolutely no reason for the mainstream Christian church to adhere to the Sunday Sabbath tradition. We can **worship** any day we want, but YHWH's **day of rest** has ALWAYS been on the seventh day. That never changed!

The idea of a Sunday sunrise resurrection connects back to Ezekiel 8:16:

*"He brought me into the inner courtyard of ADONAI's house; and there, at the entrance to the temple of ADONAI, between the porch and the altar, were about twenty five men, with their backs toward the temple of ADONAI, and their faces toward the east; and they worshipped the sun toward the east."*

Most Christians are turning their backs on Shabbat and Torah and the Word of YHWH because they follow a religion that tells them that "Jesus (and/or Paul) did away with the law." But YHWH says that He gave Torah so that His people would not turn to these things:

*Deuteronomy 4:19 "For the same reason, do not look up at the sky, at the sun, moon, stars and everything in the sky, and be drawn away to worship and serve them; Adonai your God has allotted these to all the peoples under the entire sky."*

Christians think it is acceptable to "sanctify" Sunday "in the name of Jesus" and many wouldn't think to bow before the sun and worship it; but nevertheless, they pay homage to institutions that have changed "times and laws" (Daniel 7:25) so whether Christians realize it or not, Sunday worship was ripped right out of paganism and has nothing to do with what Yeshua Himself practiced and taught.

# Chapter 7

### Acts 15 does not exempt Gentile believers from being Torah observant

---

Often, people cite Acts 15 to show that Gentiles are exempt from Torah. But, when read in context, we see an entirely different picture; one which shows that the apostles were seriously discussing which of the commandments should be the first observed by Gentile believers entering the kingdom. Let's examine just a few verses:

*Acts 15: 19 "Therefore, my opinion is that we should not put obstacles in the way of the Goyim (Gentiles) who are turning to God. 20 Instead, we should write them a letter telling them to abstain from things polluted by idols, from fornication, from what is strangled and from blood. 21 For from the earliest times, Moshe has had in every city those who proclaim him, with his words being read in the synagogues every Shabbat."*

Remember, Gentiles in Paul's day were exposed to Torah on a weekly basis at synagogue, and so Paul surmised that observation of these four rules would ultimately lead to proper obedience of **all** of the Torah. Therefore, the apostles chose the following commandments for Gentiles to begin observing which included abstaining from:

1. things polluted by idols
2. fornication
3. animals that had been strangled
4. blood

The following was borrowed and condensed from Baruch ben Daniel's article *Food* on the "Mashiyach" website.

### Abstaining from things polluted by idols:

YHWH commanded: *Exodus 20:3 "You shall have no other gods before me."*

Eating food that was dedicated to other gods shows allegiance to the people and to the god it was sacrificed to; consequently, it is forbidden.

Anyone who doesn't eat of things "sacrificed to idols" is also being careful to not convert cultural polytheistic values into a Messianic lifestyle. This is not solely about the abstention of certain foods; there are many aspects of community, and status quo values that are attached to things "sacrificed to idols."

The company a person keeps is also being addressed here; this distinction regarding food brings opportunity to introduce others to the Kingdom. This matter of eating things "sacrificed to idols" is so basic and foundational that it has the power to bring souls out of paganism, as do each of the Commandments of YHWH. To be a Kedoshim (Set Apart People), is Mashiyach (Messiah), every individual makes a choice to uphold Torah as the Word of YHWH, or not.

But false religion presents "alternatives" to the Word of YHWH; relativism, removing Set Apart distinctions to make convenient traditions so that people are not embarrassed by truth. Y'shua and his disciples never ate treif, nor things sacrificed to idols; neither would they eat "whatever" was set before them, which is simply a religious projection.

**Abstaining from fornication:**

Abstinence from fornication means avoiding every form of sexual perversion. However, the broader meaning refers to fornication with cultural deities and lifestyle choices that are rooted in paganism.

The Bride of Mashiyach has a distinct calling to be separate from paganism. The value of each soul is welcome into the Kingdom of Elohim as equals and elevated with the understanding that each one is made in "the image of Elohim." Each is called to put away "the old man," the modern evolutionary gospel that elevates man's achievements, science and religions above the Word of YHWH.

Unfortunately, there are many examples within Christianity that cater to the pagan element. For instance, Sunday church services originated with sacrifices to the sun. Easter (Ishtar) was originally a pagan festival that commemorates a sex goddess. "Easter eggs" originated in pagan fertility rituals. "Christmas trees" have their origin with Tammuz (the Branch), a sex god whose admirers put balls on small evergreen trees as testicular remembrances of their male sex god. The small evergreen tree denotes the rebirth of Tammuz.

Abstaining from fornication demands that one not practice the ways of the heathen through fornicating with their deities, or permitting syncretism to bring paganism into "the gospel".

*2 Timothy 4: 3 For the time is coming when people will not have patience for sound teaching, but will cater to their passions and gather around themselves teachers who say whatever their ears itch to hear. 4 Yes, they will stop listening to the truth, but will turn aside to follow myths. 5 But you, remain steady in every situation, endure suffering, do the work that a proclaimer of the Good News should, and do everything your service to God requires.*

## Abstaining from food that was strangled:

*Leviticus 22:8 "That which dies of itself, or is torn with beasts, he shall not eat to defile himself therewith: I am YHWH."*

*Deuteronomy 14:21 "You shall not eat of any thing that dies of itself: you shall give it unto the stranger that is in your gates, that he may eat it; or you may sell it unto an alien: for you are an holy people unto YHWH your Elohim. You shall not seethe a kid in his mother's milk."*

The commandment of not eating anything which dies of itself refers to death by natural means, regardless of how it died, it is forbidden to eat it. The commandment in Acts specifically states that the animal must not have died by strangulation, which is how some "un-kosher" butchers kill animals for food. In other words, the non-Jewish followers of Yeshua were commanded to take special precaution for where they obtained meat.

Imagine living in the days before Mashiyach, and bringing a sacrifice to the Temple to make restitution for wrong doing. Imagine taking an animal to Jerusalem for an offering during the celebration of a Feast. Treating the animal harshly, would reflect a negative attitude toward the forgiveness, grace and blessings being bestowed on you. Anyone who does not show kindness to animals, is not likely going to show kindness towards people!

The laws in Torah regarding animal welfare, are universal and timeless, because within the law are principles of Justice and Mercy that apply to all other components of life, even how we treat one another. Everything on our planet dovetails with laws that pertain to clean and unclean animals, and how we prepare our food, because they are part of YHWH's universal guidance.

The laws that pertain to animals show us that if we are to treat the blood of an animal with respect, how much more are we to respect human blood; how much more should we establish dignity for all people! There are many underlying laws and principles that enter in.

*Exodus 34:14-16 "For you shall worship no other god: for YHWH, whose name is Jealous, is a jealous Elohim: Lest you make a covenant with the inhabitants of the land, and they go a whoring after their gods, and do sacrifice unto their gods, and one call thee, and you eat of his sacrifice; And you take of their daughters unto thy sons, and their daughters go a whoring after their gods, and make thy sons go a whoring after their gods."*

A very straightforward directive, but it doesn't bode well with a Church that is embarrassed by the absolutes of the Word of YHWH. Christian sons and daughters are being instructed to go whoring after pagan gods by their priests, pastors, fathers, and mothers who "see nothing wrong" with decorating Tammuz trees for Christ-Mass, painting Ishtar eggs that commemorates a sex goddess of fertility and celebrating their gods on Sun-day. This is the modern way of fractionalizing the Word of YHWH and "eating things" sacrificed to idols.

## Abstaining from blood:

*Leviticus 7:26 "Moreover you shall eat no manner of blood, whether it be of fowl or of beast, in any of your dwellings. 27 Whatsoever soul it be that eats any manner of blood, even that soul shall be cut off from his people."*

That's very clear and for the non-Jewish followers of Yeshua:

*Leviticus 17:12 "Therefore I said unto the children of Isra'el, No soul of you shall eat blood, neither shall any stranger that sojourneth among you eat blood. 13 And whatsoever man there be of the children of Isra'el, or of the strangers that sojourn among you, which hunts and catches any beast or fowl that may be eaten; he shall even pour out the blood thereof, and cover it with dust."*

When a person "stays away from blood", they are choosing to select meat that is butchered according to the Word of YHWH. When the Torah is looked at as a whole, and we can begin to understand the unity of the Word, we can easily deduce how an animal is to be slaughtered.

Scriptures like Genesis 22:10 *"And Avraham stretched forth his hand, and took the knife to slay his son"* reveals a methodology of slaying a sacrifice. The same knife that Avraham was about to use on his own beloved son, will very shortly see its real intended purpose:

*Genesis 22: 13 "And Abraham lifted up his eyes, and looked, and behold behind him a ram caught in a thicket by his horns: and Abraham went and took the ram, and offered him up for a burnt offering in the stead of his son."*

Obviously this foreshadowed Mashiyach ben Yoseph (Messiah of Joseph), who is Yeshua; however none of us can begin to image how important that ram was to either Avraham, or his son Yitzak (Isaac)! The blood of that ram was given in exchange for his beloved son's blood; how very grateful and contrite Avraham was toward the life of that very precious ram!

110

This event holds insight for how we are to regard the life of an animal, whether for sacrifice, or for food. By showing respect for blood we are not only agreeing that blood is very important to YHWH, but that life itself is of supreme importance to the Giver of all Life!

*Genesis 9:3-6 "Every moving thing that lives shall be meat for you; even as the green herb have I given you all things. But flesh with the life thereof, which is the blood thereof, shall you not eat. And surely your blood of your lives will I require; at the hand of every beast will I require it, and at the hand of man; at the hand of every man's brother will I require the life of man. Whoso sheds man's blood, by man shall his blood be shed: for in the image of Elohim made he man."*

Yes, staying away from blood is a "negative" don't do commandment, but the positive proactive command then is to honor the life of all living creatures!

In light of the commandment to stay away from blood, the commandment to "stay away from a strangled thing" has a new progressive meaning attached to it. A strangled thing could either mean that the animal was strangled to death before it was slaughtered, or it got strangled in a fence or in a natural setting. Either way, the animal

111

did not die peacefully and the blood was not drained thoroughly.

The fact of the matter is that if the life of the animal is respected, then it is possible to slaughter it in a matter where it will die very peacefully, and not even know that it has been cut or that it is bleeding. For many, this is a difficult thing to contemplate, but of course we are not addressing vegetarians per se, but those who buy their meats from the guy across town. All who follow Yeshua, and who REALLY appreciate those summer barbecues in the park, or at the beach are commanded to "stay away from a strangled thing", no if's, but's or maybe's; therefore, the action of fulfilling this commandment draws us together in Mashiyach. Those who would defy this commandment are diverging from the Kingdom of Elohim, and the values that Mashiyach upheld with his own life!

When preparing the animal for slaughter, a person is to have a mindset that is consistent with regard to the blood of the animal. The blood and the life of the animal are synonymous, therefore the one doing the slaughter is to have an appreciation for the life he is taking, and show kindness toward the animal.

## Does Acts 15 show that Christians don't need to be circumcised?

Many Christian leaders attempt to cite Acts 15:22-35 as proof that circumcision is only for the Jews. These leaders need to re-read the words of YHWH in Genesis 17 which clearly command non-Jews who are part of Isra'el to be circumcised:

*Genesis 17: 11 You are to be cimcumcised in the flesh of your foreskin; this will be the sign of the covenant between me and you. 12 Generation after generation, every male among you who is eight days old is to be circumcised,* **including** *slaves born within your household and* **those bought from a foreigner not descended from you. 13 The slave born in your house and the person bought with your money must be circumcised; thus my covenant will be in your flesh as an everlasting covenant.** *14 Any uncircumcised male who will not let himself be circumcised in the flesh of his foreskin — that person will be cut off from his people, because he has broken my covenant."*

A footnote in the Netzari Aramaic English Interlinear explains that in Acts 15:28-29 we can see an example of binding and loosing: "The matter of circumcision was being applied commensurate to immediate need, as directed by the Ruach haKodesh (Holy Spirit). Instead of performing the act of circumcision before learning Torah, new converts are required to learn and apply Torah first, and then, when they have a good understanding, they are circumcised, but not the other way around. The keys of the Kingdom are wisdom and discernment given by the Ruach haKodesh to apply the Word of YHWH."

Yeshua, the Torah observant Jew who came to teach the world about YHWH and His Commandments, "bought and paid" for everyone including Gentiles with His own precious blood. Yeshua Himself was circumcised; therefore it stands to reason that anyone who believes in Him must also be circumcised.

# Chapter 8

## Do you still believe the "Law is a curse"?

---

*Deuteronomy 4: 39 ...know today, and establish it in your heart, that ADONAI is God in heaven above and on earth below – there is no other. 40 Therefore, **you are to keep his laws and mitzvot** which I am giving you today, so that it will go well with you and with your children after you, and so that you will prolong your days in the land ADONAI your God is giving you* **forever.**"

Please notice that verse 40 begins with "therefore" which means something very important is to follow. In this case, we are told, "you are to keep his laws and *mitzvot* (commands)....so that it will go well with you and with your children after you...." It's perfectly clear: Those who worship the God of Abraham, Isaac and Jacob MUST be Torah observant!

At the risk of being redundant, YHWH wasn't "cursing" man when He told Moses to present the Divine commandments for His people to live by! The commandments contained within Torah taught man right from wrong and showed us how to obey God and worship Him properly.

The "curse of the Law" is not the keeping of YHWH's Torah; it is our attempt to obtain salvation by following the law without faith because, as human beings, we are prone to stumble and fail at some point. ALL of His commandments were given for a reason; ALL of them were given for our benefit. He didn't, after the Creation, throw Man out into a pasture to fend for himself; He gave us a divine blueprint for holy living.

Yet many Christians refuse to even bother with the Ten Commandments, let alone the "613", insisting "Jesus gave us just two to follow":

*Matthew 22: 37 He told him, "You are to love Adonai your God with all your heart and with all your soul and with all your strength. 38 This is the greatest and most important mitzvah. 39 And a second is similar to it, 'You are to love your neighbor as yourself.' 40 All of the Torah and the Prophets are dependent on these two mitzvoth."*

Does the above in any way suggest the other commands are now null and void? Please note and contemplate verse 40: Does it say you can now IGNORE the Law and the Prophets? If those are the only two commandments to follow, the question remains: How do we know not to lie, murder, steal, commit adultery, etc.? From our parents? Our friends? Whom? And where did they find out how to behave in a Godly manner? The answer is: YHWH was the first One to present the rules of moral, Godly

116

conduct – and there were certainly more than two! He graced us with many, revealing them according to His own desires and in His own good timing – and He expected them to be followed without question!

Ask anyone on the street to cite the Ten Commandments – or even just the "two" and see what happens. You will surely be hard-pressed to find even one who could provide a straight answer. Our society's absence of morality and penchant for "tolerance" and "acceptance" of ungodly behavior is ample evidence of that fact!

Matthew 22: 37-40, read in context, means that if we love God with all our hearts, we will do whatever it takes to follow His Torah. The following is a footnote from the Netzari Aramaic English Interlinear by Andrew Gabriel Roth:

> "The Torah and Prophets hang or 'hold on by' these two great commandments of Love. Those who do the Commandments, are they who love YHWH (Matt 19:17; 1 John 5:2-3). Without love, observance of Torah is vanity, and without Torah, one's 'love' is vanity."

Without YHWH's divine instructions, Man is totally lost! There were and are and always will be parts of Torah which God said would endure FOREVER....

Second Timothy 3:16 says, *"All scripture is God-breathed and is valuable for teaching the truth, convicting of sin, correcting faults and training in right living"*....

This verse from the *Brit Chadasha* (New Testament) says "ALL scripture is God-breathed"; it doesn't say, "All scripture except for the Torah...."

The Tanakh ("Old Testament") shows over and over that, in Biblical times, if a Gentile joined him or herself to Isra'el, they were required to give up their former pagan ways. The Bible states that there is **one** Torah for Isra'el and the Gentile who dwells with her. YHWH explicitly said:

*Exodus 12: 49 "The same teaching is to apply equally to the citizen and to the foreigner living among you."*

In other words: As believers in the God of Abraham, Isaac and Jacob, we are one in God's eyes, and are therefore required to act accordingly.

*Leviticus 17: 8 "Also tell them, 'When someone from the community of Isra'el or one of the foreigners living with you offers a burnt offering or sacrifice 9 without bringing it to the entrance of the tent of meeting to sacrifice it to ADONAI, that person is to be cut off from his people.*

*Numbers 9: 14 If a foreigner is staying with you and wants to observe Pesach (Passover) for ADONAI, he is to do it according to the regulations and rules of Pesach — you are to have the same law for the foreigner as for the citizen of the land.'"*

*Deuteronomy 31: 12 "Assemble the people — the men, the women, the little ones and the foreigners you have in your towns — so that they can hear, learn, fear ADONAI your God and take care to obey all the words of this Torah; 13 and so*

118

*that their children, who have not known, can hear and learn to fear ADONAI your God, for as long as you live in the land you are crossing the Yarden to possess."*

## Something to think about:

*Deuteronomy 32: 21 They aroused my jealousy with a non-god and provoked me with their vanities; I will arouse their jealousy with a non-people and provoke them with a vile nation.*

In the Tanakh the words "gentile", "heathen" and "pagan" were often synonymous. A Gentile was (and still is) a non-Jew, someone who did/does not believe in, or worship YHWH. (Please see Ezra 6:21, Nehemiah 5:8-9, Isaiah 9:1, 42:6.)

*Romans 10: 19 "But, I say, isn't it rather that Isra'el didn't understand?" "I will provoke you to jealousy over a non-nation, over a nation void of understanding I will make you angry."*

Those who are a "non-nation" are Gentiles, not Christians! Christians aren't a "nation"....

*Romans 11: 11 "In that case, I say, isn't it that they have stumbled with the result that they have permanently fallen away?" Heaven forbid! Quite the contrary, it is by means of their stumbling that the deliverance has come to the Gentiles, in order to provoke them to jealousy.*

Please note Paul, a Jew, does not say "Christians" or "the Church" will be grafted in or provoke Jews to jealousy; he said "Gentiles." In other words, it won't be the Christians through one of their myriad Torah-less denominations who end up making the Jews jealous; it will be the Torah observant believers in Messiah....

*Zechariah 8: 23 ADONAI-Tzva'ot says, 'When that time comes, ten men will take hold – speaking all the languages of the nations – will grab hold of the cloak of a Jew and say, "We want to go with you, because we have heard that God is with you."'*

Gentiles are "grafted in" to the Olive Tree. It's the JEWS - the ones with whom YHWH made His original covenant - who are doing the sharing of the "rich root of the olive tree," not the Gentiles - but the Torah observant Gentile believers in Messiah will certainly get to play a major part:

*Romans 11: 17 But if some of the branches were broken off, and you – a wild olive – were grafted in among them and have become equal sharers in the rich root of the olive tree then don't boast as if you were better than the branches! However, if you do boast, remember that you are not supporting the root, the root is supporting you.*

So, if anyone will lead the Jews to jealousy, it's those who are Torah observant believers in Yeshua haMashiyach - those who have put away their weak flesh and drawn close to YHWH and His Messiah by actually "walking out" God's will. Those who insist this is being "legalistic" don't realize **they** are the ones who are totally off the mark because the Bible, over and over again, refers to our need to be Torah observant:

*Joshua 1: 8 Do not let this **Book of the Law** depart from your mouth; meditate on it day and night, so that you may be careful to **do everything written in it**. Then you will be prosperous and successful.*

As has been reiterated over and over again in this book, Yeshua was a Torah observant, Sabbath and feast-keeping, kosher Jew who was foreshadowed throughout the Tanakh and came to be our final Sin Sacrifice. To try to separate Him from His Jewishness makes about as much sense as separating Martin Luther King from his African-American heritage!

*Genesis 49: 10 The scepter will not pass from Y'hudah, nor the ruler's staff from between his legs, until he comes to whom [obedience] belongs; and it is he whom the peoples will obey.*

Although this whole concept is certainly a hard pill to swallow for those God-fearing Christians who love the Lord with all their hearts, you must ask yourself this: Why would the Jews want to drop Torah and everything they've ever believed of their Tanakh in order to follow (the Christian) "Jesus" who in no way resembles the God of Abraham, Isaac and Jacob?

Yeshua Himself commanded us to spread the Gospel (Matthew 28:18) and Rav Sha'ul (Apostle Paul) later spoke of the Gentiles making the Jews "jealous" (Romans 10:19, 11:11 and 11:14 – which fulfilled Deuteronomy 32:21). We MUST spread the Good News; but we must do it according to YHWH's commands!

Although there are already many Jews whose spiritual eyes have been opened to the Truth of Messiah, the eyes of most traditional Jews are still blinded for now (but not for much longer because, judging from world events, especially in the Middle East, we are in the end times as outlined in the Books of Daniel and Revelation). YHWH scattered His chosen people for the purpose of spreading the word about Himself. If it hadn't been for the believing Jews, the world would never have heard of YHWH or Yeshua! He would have remained the best-kept secret of tiny, little Isra'el, and the rest of the world would still be drowning in paganism, unaware of the Torah or the Messiah.

Keeping in mind everything you've read here; please remember that in spreading the Gospel it is an absolute death knell to approach traditional Jews with words like: "Jesus loves you; He died for you and while He was at it, He nailed the law to the cross so you don't have to perform 'works' anymore – and if you don't believe this, you'll go to hell." (Only YHWH Himself will decide who will or won't be in Heaven with Him!) Why would Jews want to worship someone who seems to contradict the entire Tanakh and who supposedly superseded His own forever commands – and whose followers, the "Christians," have been killing Jews since time immemorial in an effort to force them to "accept Jesus into their hearts"?

A well-known evangelist recently suggested that in the end of days Jews will eventually become

Christians; while a well-known and popular author commented that the U.S. would be a better place if there weren't any Jewish people and that they needed to "perfect" themselves by becoming Christians.

Both comments stem from complete ignorance! Jews will never "become Christians" and the U.S. has been blessed, in part, BECAUSE of the presence of YHWH's "Chosen People." While most Jews haven't yet realized that their promised Messiah has already come and will soon return, they DO know who "God" is and they know He has promised that He will always take care of them:

Jeremiah 31: 34(35) *This is what ADONAI says, who gives the sun as light for the day, who ordained the laws for the moon and stars to provide light for the night, who stirs up the sea until its waves roar – ADONAI-Tzva'ot is his name: 35(36) "If these laws leave my presence," says ADONAI, "then the offspring of Isra'el will stop being a nation in my presence forever." 36(37) This is what ADONAI says: "If the sky above can be measured and the foundations of the earth be fathomed, then I will reject all the offspring of Isra'el for all that they have done," says ADONAI.*

Religious Jews are Torah observant and doing His will already - which certainly puts them in a favorable light with Him! But so far, they haven't been willing to acknowledge they already have a Final Sin Sacrifice in Yeshua. However, the Bible tells us they **will** one day:

Romans 11: 25 *"For, brothers, I want you to understand this truth which God formerly concealed but has now revealed, so*

123

*that you won't imagine you know more than you actually do.*
*It is that stoniness, to a degree, has come upon Isra'el, until*
*the Gentile world enters in its fullness; 26 and that it is in this*
*way that all Isra'el will be saved. As the Tanakh says, "Out*
*of Tzion will come the Redeemer; he will turn away*
*ungodliness from Ya'akov and this will be my covenant with*
*them... when I take away their sins."*

YHWH as our Creator can offer eternal life to anyone
He wants, and so no human has a right to decide who
will or will not end up in heaven. In the meantime,
believers must band together to show not only our
Jewish brethren, but the entire world that Yeshua said
NO ONE comes to the Father except through Him:

*John 14: 6 "I AM the Way - and the Truth and the Life; no*
*one comes to the Father except through me.*

The apostle Paul settled the matter long ago when he
said:

*Romans 1:16: For I am not ashamed of the Good News, since*
*it is God's powerful means of bringing salvation to everyone*
*who keeps on trusting, to the Jew especially, but equally to the*
*Gentile.*

Yeshua Himself told His disciples to spread the Good
News:

*Matthew 28: 19 Therefore, go and make people from all*
*nations into talmidim (disciples), immersing them into the*
*reality of the Father, the Son, and the Ruach haKodesh, 20*
*and teaching them to* **obey everything that I have**

**commanded you**. *And remember! I will be with you always, yes, even until the end of the age.*"

As suggested at the beginning of this book, if you want to be a good steward of God's Word and you desire to witness to a lost world including your Jewish brethren, forget about what your pastor has been teaching you and see for yourself what the Bible actually says! Hopefully, now you can see why....

Also, remember I asked you to keep in mind the words of the prophet Micah who asked: *"With what can I come before ADONAI to bow down before God on high?"* (Micah 6: 6)

If you're one of the few who has actually grasped the concept of Torah in your journey through this book, then the answer to Micah's question should have been crystal clear: "My total obedience to Him and His Torah! No more excuses, no more willingness to follow man's ideology or theology, and no more paganism!"

*Psalms 119: 33 Teach me, ADONAI, the way of your laws; keeping them will be its own reward for me. 34 Give me understanding; then I will keep your Torah; I will observe it with all my heart. (The obedience gained through Torah.)*

As sad as it might sound, because of their refusal to accept Torah, Christian pastors have renounced being holy and "Set Apart" unto YHWH, as this requires following in the footsteps of Mashiyach who led by example to show us how to do it.

To most Christians being "holy" means to be embedded in a church where belief in their particular theology is required (in most churches you can't become a member unless you sign an agreement that you adhere to their theology) and to join in whatever that church is doing to "win souls" and help it grow to enormous proportions by perpetuating "ear tickling" doctrine. Is this really what you want to offer YHWH on Judgment Day – to tell Him, "Lord, I did all this for You"? Or would you rather be able to stand before Him and proclaim: "Abba Father, I did it Your way!"

*Matthew 7: 21 Not everyone who says to me 'Lord, Lord' will enter the Kingdom of Heaven,* **only those who do what my Father in heaven wants** *(i.e.: Torah) 22 On that Day, many will say to me, 'Lord, Lord! Didn't we prophesy in your name? Didn't we expel demons in your name? Didn't we perform many miracles in your name?' 23 Then I will tell them to their faces, 'I never knew you! Get away from me, you workers of lawlessness!'* (i.e., they did not keep Torah --- they were lawless – without the Law!)

**A word of warning:** IF, you are among the few who has fully grasped the concept of Torah, and IF, as a result, you decide to become Torah observant, be prepared for some major persecution from those who cannot or will not see. It has been my experience that most Christians will fight you to the death over the idea of "the law". Once the persecution comes, all you can do is to cling to the Word and ask yourself: "Whom will I follow – God or mammon?" In those trying times it will be imperative to remember the words of Yeshua who said:

*Matthew 10: 21 A brother will betray his brother to death, and a father his child; children will turn against their parents and have them put to death. 22 Everyone will hate you because of me, but whoever holds out till the end will be preserved from harm.*

*Matthew 10: 34 "Don't suppose that I have come to bring peace to the land. It is not peace I have come to bring, but a sword! 35 For I have come to set 36 a man against his father, a daughter against her mother, a daughter-in-law against her mother-in-law, so that a man's enemies will be the members of his own household.*

*Matthew 10: 37 Whoever loves his father or mother more than he loves me is not worthy of me; anyone who love his son or daughter more than he loves me is not worthy of me. 38 And anyone who does not take up his execution-stake and follow me is not worthy of me. 39 Whoever finds his own life will lose it, but the person who loses his life for my sake will find it.*

## Some final thoughts:

*Zechariah 13: 4 When that day comes, each one of the prophets will be shamed by his vision when he prophesies. He will stop wearing a hair cloak to deceive people; 5 and instead, he will say, 'I'm no prophet, I just work the soil; since my youth I've only wanted to be an ordinary man.' 6 If someone asks him, 'Then what are these gashes between your shoulders?' he will answer, 'I got hurt at my friend's house.' 7 "Awake, sword, against my shepherd, against the man who is close to me," says Adonai-Tzva'ot. "Strike the shepherd, and the sheep will be scattered; I will turn my hand against the young ones. 8 In time, throughout that land," says Adonai, "two-thirds of those in it will be destroyed – they will die, but one-third will remain. 9 That third part I will bring through the fire; I will refine them as silver is refined, I will test them as gold is tested. They will call on my name, and I will answer them, I will say, 'This is my people' and they will say, 'Adonai is my God.'"*

Notice that two parts get wiped out and then the third part goes through the Refiner! Are YOU ready? Or are you going to keep worshipping YHWH according to the ways of Man? Mashiyach Yeshua brought a GOVERNMENT, not a religion and many will come to realize in these latter days that His Government will test, try and shake out everything that is not of YHWH. My prayer for all of you is that you would drop all man-made ideas and begin to follow the One who created you!

*Romans 7: 7 Therefore, what are we to say? That the Torah is sinful? Heaven forbid! Rather, the function of the Torah was that without it, I would not have known what sin is. For example, I would not have become conscious of what greed is if the Torah had not said, "Thou shalt not covet."*

*Romans 7: 12 So the Torah is holy; that is, the commandment is holy, just and good.*

The following is a quote from Baruch ben Daniel's website "Mashiyach" in an article entitled, "The Sanctuary or the Church":

The fact of the matter is that Christian Pastors have NO Fear of YHWH; they've been trained according to a pagan hierarchy to fear man, and climb the christo-political ladder. The Seminary gave them "credentials" and "better doctrine" than other denominations, so with the backing of some "reformer" or institution, who needs the real Mashiyach? As long as people keep coming back every Sunday or Sabbath, the Pastor feels he must be doing something right.

Christians who actually read their Bibles and are honest with themselves, already know that the Church is on the other side of a great gulf. It's nearly impossible to bridge the gulf between the Kingdom of Elohim and false religious traditions because the church is so deeply entrenched into a pagan value system, culture and government that breaks Torah.

... One of the most famous sayings of Pastors is, "it's not for today", or "Yes, I would love to enjoy Shabbat" or "Yes, the Feasts are awesome" but yet they put up their Tammuz trees, and paint their Ishtar eggs, because people will leave their churches if they are not given that old time Christian religion. Gutless pastors are the vast majority; they are hirelings who lead an apostate fallen religious system that plagues the earth....

Why would anyone want to put their trust in any other than Mashiyach? What a foolish game to play when people look to their Rabbi or Pastor or Guru as a hero of truth. YHWH warned us through John to "come out of her my people" and he wasn't talking about the bingo halls! It is very clear about the Testimony of Yeshua, "Blessed are they that do His commandments, that they may have right to the Tree of Life, and may enter in through the gates into the city. For without are dogs, and sorcerers, and whoremongers, and murderers, and idolaters, and whosoever loves and makes a lie."

I pray the words of this book have caused you to rethink what you have been taught in your churches. Although I already used this in a previous chapter, I want to close with these thoughts from Andrew Gabriel Roth, which beautifully sum up the whole idea behind, "Should Christians be Torah Observant?"... specifically answering the question as to what was nailed to the cross:

"So when we are guilty of sin, YHWH is one witness to that guilt, and the record that is generated of that sin is another. However, with the reconcilement of Y'shua on the cross dying in our place, that second witness/record against us is obliterated, and the Torah remains simply to guide us in the path of righteousness for the rest of our redeemed lives."

# Appendix 1

## The Biblical Feasts and their eternal significance

---

*Isaiah 66: 22 For just as the new heavens and the new earth that I am making will continue in my presence," says ADONAI, "so will your descendants and your name continue. 23 "Every month on Rosh-Hodesh (new moon to new moon) and every week on Shabbat, **everyone living** will come to worship in my presence," says ADONAI.*

The fact that all flesh will one day worship YHWH according to His calendar also tells us that the Biblical Feasts/appointed times) are not only for Jews, but for all who worship the God of Abraham, Isaac and Jacob.

YHWH's *mo'adim*, the Biblical feasts – the "fixed" or "appointed" times listed and described in Leviticus 23, were instituted by YHWH Himself to be set apart times for Israel to gather and worship the Holy One. Each feast foreshadows Yeshua (who has so far fulfilled the first four of the seven) and plays a major part in prophecy.

As you will see in the following pages which briefly outline the feasts, these days occur at varying times on our Gregorian calendar because man's timetable/calendar is different from God's.

**Passover/Pesach** (Nisan 14) always falls in the March/April timeframe on the Gregorian calendar: Leviticus 23:5 tells us: *"In the first month, on the fourteenth day of the month, between sundown and complete darkness, comes Pesach for ADONAI."*

This Feast celebrates the deliverance of the Hebrew slaves from Egypt. It is a tale of redemption through the killing of the Passover Lamb whose blood was to be applied to the doorposts of their houses – an act which would spare their firstborn from the Tenth Curse against Pharaoh. YHWH promised that the Angel of Death would "pass over" those houses with the blood on the doorposts, and spare the first born (Exodus 12:1-13).

This foreshadowed Yeshua, YHWH's "Passover Lamb" who fulfilled Passover when he was crucified and willingly allowed His own blood to be shed on our behalf in order to become our redemption. In other words, the innocent died for the guilty; and sacrifice not only means death but also life (Isaiah 53.)

During the celebration of Passover, we are not only to remember but to identify with the bitterness of slavery and the speed of the exodus by eating bitter herbs and matzah (unleavened bread).

(As an aside, not only were the Israelites led out of Egypt and given physical liberation on 14 Nisan (Exodus 12:1-13) which foreshadowed Yeshua, THE Passover Lamb whose death provided spiritual liberation [see Matthew, Mark, Luke and John], but also, many of the European concentration camps were liberated on or around 14 Nisan, and Hitler committed suicide during this timeframe [April 30, 1945]. Coincidence?)

**Unleavened Bread/Hag HaMatzot** (Nisan 15) marks the beginning of a seven day period during which the eating of leavened Bread is forbidden as leaven is a symbol of sin (1 Corinthians 5:6-8, Matthew 16:11-12, Galatians 5:7-9). Messiah Yeshua fulfilled this Feast when he was buried and became our righteousness (Romans 6:4, 2 Corinthians 5:21).

Exodus 23:14-16 says:

*"Three times a year, you are to observe a festival for me. Keep the festival of matzah: for seven days, as I ordered you, you are to eat matzah at the time determined in the month of Aviv; for it was in that month that you left Egypt. No one is to appear before me empty-handed. Next, the festival of harvest, the first fruits of your efforts sowing in the field; and last, the festival of ingathering, at the end of the year, when you gather in from the fields the results of your efforts."*

**Firstfruits/Yom HaBikkurim** (Nisan 16) falls during the March/April timeframe: This Feast, celebrating the bringing of the firstfruits of the winter harvest to the Temple (indicating there will be more to come!) is symbolic of Yeshua being the Firstfruits (1 Corinthians 15:23). His resurrection was a "wave offering" presented to YHWH as the firstfruits of the harvest of souls that is yet to come.

**Feast of Weeks/Shavuot** (known by Christians as "Pentecost") is celebrated during the May/June timeframe. Exodus 34:22 tells us: *"Observe the festival of Shavuot with the first-gathered produce of the wheat harvest, and the festival of ingathering at the turn of the year...."*

Shavuot falls fifty days after Passover. Torah directs the seven-week Counting of the Omer (which begins on the second day of Passover and culminates after seven weeks, the next day being Shavuot). The counting of the days and weeks conveys anticipation of and desire for the Giving of the Torah. In other words, at Passover, the Israelites were freed from slavery in Egypt; and 50 days later on Shavuot they accepted YHWH's Torah which made them a nation committed to serving God.

This Feast was fulfilled by the coming of the promised Ruach HaKodesh (Holy Spirit) on the disciples of Yeshua in the Temple. It represents the beginning of the body of Messiah on Earth in which all believers, redeemed through the blood of Messiah, are lifted up before ADONAI and set apart as holy (Acts 2, John 14:15-18, Ephesians 2:11-22).

During this time, believers read the book of Ruth (King David's grandmother and an ancestor of Yeshua), which is the story of a non-Jew who was accepted into the household of Isra'el.

**Trumpets/Rosh Hashana** (Tishri 1) falls in the September/October timeframe: Leviticus 23:23-25 says:

*ADONAI said to Moshe, "Tell the people of Isra'el, 'In the seventh month, the first of the month is to be for you a day of complete rest for remembering, a holy convocation announced with blasts on the shofar. Do not do any kind of ordinary work, and bring an offering made by fire to ADONAI.'"*

It is the Jewish New Year; the anniversary of the creation of Adam and Eve and their first actions toward the realization of man's role in the world; of the first sin that was committed and resulting repentance; a day when YHWH takes stock of His Creation, which includes all of humanity. During this Feast, the blowing of shofars (rams' horns) signifies the bringing together of God's people, warning them to repent during the coming "days of awe" (the 10 days between Trumpets and the Day of Atonement).

According to tradition, during this time the Jewish people concentrate all their efforts into making amends with their brethren and apologizing for past offenses. However, what most traditional Jews do not yet realize is that this Feast is the next one to be fulfilled by Yeshua - when the trumpets sound and the true believers in Messiah Yeshua are gathered/resurrected (I Thessalonians 4:13-18, I Corinthians 15:50-54).

The Feast of Trumpets also signals the call for repentance, for the time is short and Judgment is coming upon the Earth – whether people are ready, or not! (See the Book of Revelation.)

**Day of Atonement/Yom Kippur** (Tishri 10) falls in the September/October timeframe: Leviticus 16:29-31 tells us:

*"It is to be a permanent regulation for you that on the tenth day of the seventh month you are to deny yourselves and not to do any kind of work, both the citizen and the foreigner living with you. For on this day, atonement will be made for you to purify you; you will be clean before ADONAI from all your sins. It is a Shabbat of complete rest for you, and you are to deny yourselves. This is a permanent regulation."*

This Feast represents the need for the sacrifice/sin offering that must be made for the sins of the nation. We're told that Yeshua shall descend to put to an end to the sins of Isra'el who, at that time will call for the Messiah to return and will mourn for the "One who was pierced". This day will be fulfilled upon the Second Coming of Messiah to the Earth (Matthew 23:37-39, Hosea 5:15 thru 6:1-3, Zecheriah 13:8, 9 Zecheriah 12:10, Zecheriah 13:1, Ezekiel 16:61-63).

**Tabernacles/Sukkot** (Tishri 15) falls in the September/October timeframe. This Feast is outlined in Deuteronomy 16:13-15, where YHWH tells the Israelites:

*"You are to keep the festival of Sukkot for seven days after you have gathered the produce of your threshing-floor and winepress. Rejoice at your festival – you, your sons and daughters, your male and female slaves, the L'vi'im (Levites), and the foreigners, orphans and widows living among you. Seven days you are to keep the festival for ADONAI your God in the place ADONAI your God will choose, because ADONAI your God will bless you in all your crops and in all your work, so you are to be full of joy!*

Leviticus 23:39-43 says:

*"'But on the fifteenth day of the seventh month, when you have gathered the produce of the land, you are to observe the festival of ADONAI seven days; the first day is to be a complete rest and the eighth day is to be a complete rest. On the first day you are to take choice fruit, palm fronds, thick branches and river-willows, and celebrate in the presence of ADONAI your God for seven days. You are to observe it as a feast to ADONAI seven days in the year; it is a permanent regulation, generation after generation; keep it in the seventh month. You are to live in sukkot for seven days; every citizen of Isra'el is to live in a sukkah, so that generation after generation of you will know that I made the people of Isra'el live in sukkot when I brought them out of the land of Egypt; I am ADONAI your God.'"*

Did you notice that ALL Isra'el is to live in a sukkah for seven days? (This includes Christian believers, because YHWH gave us ONE covenant, not two separate ones in which Gentiles are exempt from keeping Torah. We all worship the same God...)

This Feast serves as a reminder of the days in the wilderness when YHWH's people were forced to reside in tents/huts or temporary dwellings – a reminder of our temporary lives on Earth. It will be fulfilled by the ingathering of the "Final Harvest" of souls just prior to the setting up of the Kingdom of the Messiah on Earth.

Philippians 2:10-11 tells us in that day Yeshua will reign from Jerusalem and *"every knee will bow in heaven, on earth and under the earth – and every tongue will acknowledge that Yeshua the Messiah is ADONAI – to the glory of God the Father."* His Kingdom is to last 1,000 years before the eternal order begins in the "new heaven and new earth" (Revelation 21)!

If you're still unsure that Christians are supposed to observe these feasts, please read Leviticus 25:6-47.

Each place in Torah that refers to "stranger" or "sojourner" speaks to those who were not born as Jews or Israelites but have chosen to join themselves to YHWH and His people, to be One people. YHWH even refers to Himself as a sojourner with His people!

Not only is the entire plan of Salvation illustrated in the *mo'adim*, but through observing each set time one begins to live within the timetable of YHWH's Word. The *mo'adim* are some of the most powerful ways we can learn and also teach our children about life and what it means....

# Appendix 2

## Concerning the "Trinity"

The word "Trinity" is not found anywhere in Scripture. While the Bible never actually uses the term "Trinity" we have indeed seen YHWH as Father, Son, and Holy Spirit. But, He has also revealed Himself through a burning bush, as pillars of cloud and fire, as "three men" to Abraham at the Oaks of Mamre, and He even spoke through a donkey. So, calling Him a "Trinity" is actually limiting Him....

The mere fact that YHWH revealed Himself to us in plural aspects shows that He is a plurality – however, this plurality should in no way be seen in the form of a "Person" or "Persons" because, again, this limits the Creator (more on that later):

*Isaiah 48:12 "Listen to me Ya'akov; Isra'el whom I have called: I am he who is first; I am also the last."....*

*Isaiah 48:16 "Come close to me and listen to this: since the beginning I have not spoken in secret, since the time things began to be, I have been there; and now Adonai Elohim has sent me and his Spirit."*

Furthermore John 1 tells us:   *1 In the beginning was the Word, and the Word was with God, and the Word was God. 2 He was with God in the beginning. 3 All things came to be through him, and without him nothing made had being. 4 In him was life, and the life was the light of mankind. 5 The light shines in the darkness, and the darkness not has suppressed it.*

Also, YHWH constantly referred to Himself in the plural form, including the use of "US" and "WE".

*Genesis 1: 26 Then God said, "Let Us make humankind in Our image, in the likeness of ourselves;;* (Note - He did NOT say "likenesses").

When traditional Jews recite the "Shema" ("Listen/Hear"), they say, "Hear O Isra'el, the Lord our God, the Lord is One." The Hebrew word used for "One" in this case is ECHAD which is a plural form of "one" (as in ONE DOZEN eggs, or ONE BUNCH of grapes, or when a couple marries they become ONE unit). Back in Biblical times, whenever they spoke of just one singular item – such as one egg, or one grape - they used the term YACHID.

YHWH appeared to Abraham in the form of a man – actually, as THREE men (but not a "trinity"):

*Genesis 18:  1 Adonai appeared to Avraham by the oaks of Mamre as he sat at the entrance to the tent during the heat of the day. 2 He raised his eyes and looked, and there in front of him stood three men. On seeing them, he ran from the tent door to meet them, prostrated himself on the ground....*

YHWH is an "Echad" who also revealed Himself to us in the form of a "Son":

*Proverbs 30: 4 Who has gone up to heaven and come down? Who has cupped the wind in the palms of his hands? Who has wrapped up the waters in his cloak? Who established all the ends of the earth? What is his name, and what is his son's name? Surely you know!*

Whenever I attempt to illustrate God to atheists or those who have problems with the fact that He was running the universe while at the same time walking the Earth as someone called "Jesus," I use the following example:

Imagine a fiber optics lamp with thousands of tiny fibers emanating light. Note that these fibers are connected to one single Base. YHWH can be likened to the Base of that lamp, which is the actual Power or Source. The little fibers are all a part of that Power, and Yeshua can be likened to one of those fibers. He was but ONE aspect of YHWH, eternally connected to YHWH; thus, He was "YHWH in the Flesh" while He walked the Earth. That does not mean that while Yeshua walked the Earth, YHWH was no longer in charge of the universe; Yeshua isn't the "Base" – YHWH is! The "Base" controls everything and everything is dependent upon that Base. How YHWH chooses to reveal Himself to us is up to Him, but we cannot limit Him by insisting He is a "trinity."

The following is a capsulated version of author Baruch ben Daniel's article, "YHWH Revealed in Mashiyach":

> The spiritual nature of YHWH is hard to grasp via our limited, human mindsets. Part of the problem rests with the personification of "spirits". In the pagan world "ghosts" are given pet names and personalities, and this ideology has been applied to the One True Elohim, but the truth is that YHWH is One Spirit, not many. The Spirit of YHWH is YHWH, He is not a "person", and cannot be categorized by man's numerical or limited dimensional being.

> *1 Corinthians 3:16, 17 – "Don't you know that you are the temple of Elohim, and that the Spirit of Elohim dwells in you? If any man defile the temple of Elohim, him shall Elohim destroy; for the temple of Elohim is holy, which temple ye are."*

> The people of YHWH have the Spirit of Elohim within them, and every human soul also has a unique human spirit.

> *John 3: 6 "That which is born of the flesh is flesh; and that which is born of the Spirit is spirit."*

> Persons of the "Trinity" is complex; a "person" has an intellect, emotions, a will, a physical body and a spirit; so to say

"persons" of the Trinity is very problematic, simply because YHWH is not a "person". You are a "person" and I am a "person". We do find that in Torah, the Neviim (Prophets), the Ketuvim Netzarim (writings of the Jewish Disciples) the writers stress that YHWH is Echad, He is ONE. So, although the word "Trinity" might suffice as a harmless and quick reference to the Godhead as Father, Son and Holy Spirit, it is not so innocent a doctrine if one insists there are three "persons" of the "Trinity". Truth can be transformed into idolatry if we are not extremely careful to base our values and understanding on Scripture.

Yeshua is the Arm of YHWH revealed as God who came in the flesh and is part of what we understand as "the Godhead" but there is no need to imagine two or three beings or persons within "the Godhead" as this kind of thinking is pagan in origin. It wasn't until +/- 220 AD that a Greek thinker named Tertullian coined the term "Trinity" after reading Philo who coined the word "Triad". By 375 AD martyrdom over the theology of "the Trinity" was well under way in Western Christianity, but it wasn't until the 12th century that the Church of the East also began to use the term.

Philo got his ideas from "Metatron" or what was then the oral Kabbalah which referred to

Mashiyach as the "middle pillar" which harmonizes all the Attributes of YHWH as One. Mashiyach came into time and space, but his Father YHWH exists outside of time and space. When Mashiyach was revealed as the Arm of YHWH we saw "the Father" but we did not and could not possibly see all dimensions of YHWH's power and might! How can finite beings input infinite data into our minds and spirits? It's not possible, but it is possible for Mashiyach, the "Anointed of YHWH" to reveal the Father to us within time and space.

You have a spirit, you have a mind and body, but one would never separate your spirit from your soul as though they are two different beings; this is where the Church fell into paganism, because the ideas were brought into the Faith of Yeshua by polytheistic pagans.

# Appendix 3

## Concerning "Kosher" Foods

The idea of "clean and unclean" animals was postulated to Man right from the very beginning:

*Genesis 7: 8 Of clean animals, of animals that are not clean, of birds, and of everything that creeps on the ground, 9 couples, male and female, went into Noach in the ark, as God had ordered Noach.*

YHWH outlined for us in the Book of Leviticus what He considered to be food – and that has **never** changed! **All** believers are to eat only kosher foods which meet the criteria of Torah. ("Kosher" is the set of dietary laws governing what can or cannot be consumed).

*Leviticus 11: 1 ADONAI said to Moshe and Aharon, 2 "Tell the people of Isra'el, 'These are the living creatures which you may eat among all the land animals....*

Leviticus 11:3 describes "clean" animals as those that have cloven hooves and chew their cud; while Leviticus 11:4 warns that, unless the animals chew their cud and have cloven hooves, they would be considered "unclean".

The "unclean" animals are those that are carnivorous, eating raw dead and diseased creatures and/or things that, if they were ingested by a ordinary human being, would kill us. The impurities and poisons – while they don't kill the "unclean" birds and animals who eat them – are absorbed into their systems; and if we then turn around and eat those "unclean" birds or animals, their impurities and poisons are further absorbed into OUR systems.

*Leviticus 11: 4-6 But you are not to eat those that only chew the cud or only have a separate hoof. For example, the camel, the coney, and the hare are unclean for you, because they chew the cud but don't have a separate hoof; 7 while the pig is unclean for you, because, although it has a separate and completely divided hoof, it doesn't chew the cud. 8 You are not to eat meat from these or touch their carcasses; they are unclean for you.*

Leviticus 11:9-12 describes kosher and unkosher seafood, and from there YHWH continues a painstaking description of exactly what kinds of foods He wanted us to either eat or abstain from. And who was He talking to? Isra'el! Who is Isra'el? Anyone who believes in the God of Abraham, Isaac and Jacob! So, what's not to understand?

Yet, there are people who insist that Yeshua, Paul and others said we could eat whatever we want, meaning there is no more "kosher" because of verses such as the below....

*Mark 7: 18 He replied to them, "So you too are without understanding? Don't you see that nothing going into a person from outside can make him unclean? 19 For it doesn't go into his heart but into his stomach, and it passes out into the latrine." (Thus he declared all foods ritually clean.)*

Mark 7 showcases one of the greatest discussions of oral versus written Jewish law that exists in New Covenant writings. In many ways this presages the heated exchanges that would be recorded in the Talmud some 200 years later. However, a major misunderstanding of this verse found its way into the modern translations with the parenthetical comment, "Thus Yeshua declared all foods ritually clean." Neither Aramaic nor early Greek manuscripts include this in the text, which is clearly an attempt by Gentile editors to abandon Torah's dietary laws.

The point being established is that if you plot things like murder, lies, adulteries and so forth, then why be concerned about the food you eat, when weightier things are making you much more unclean than your food. Even if a person kept a perfectly kosher diet, but had such unclean thoughts, they would rank among the most unkosher of people. (See Luke 11:40.)

*1 Timothy 4:: 1 The Spirit expressly states that in the acharit-hayamim some people will apostatize from the faith by paying attention to deceiving spirits and things taught by demons. 2 Such teachings come from the hypocrisy of liars whose own consciences have been burned, as if with a red-hot branding iron. 3 They forbid marriage and require abstinence from foods which God created to be eaten with thanksgiving by those who have come to trust and to know the truth. 4 For everything created by God is good, and nothing received with thanksgiving needs to be rejected, 5 because the word of God and prayer make it holy.*

In the above, did Paul say, "since Jesus nailed it to the cross, we can eat whatever we want"?  No!

First of all we have to remember that Paul – a mere man who was kosher himself – was talking to the Jews – who were all kashrut/kosher already. They wouldn't dream of going against what God said in Leviticus about what He considered to be food!

Paul warned against doctrines of demons which say you can't have certain foods which God has said are good to eat.  Every edible creature is good and not to be refused **if** it is made holy by the Word of God and prayer (thanksgiving).  Leviticus is the Word of God, and it describes for us what is holy and not holy. That is what kosher actually means, as it comes from the same root as kodesh, meaning holy.

For those who insist, "Kosher is only for the Jews!" I would ask them to contemplate whether or not the biology of the human body differs between Jews and Gentiles. Yeshua was a Jew, and we never see any instances that reveal that He ever consumed pork. Pork and seafood, raw or improperly prepared, will kill a Jew just as fast as a Gentile, and vice-versa.

YHWH had a reason for imposing rules and regulations on us, and since He said "Don't eat this or that" our job is not to question but to obey....

The Books of Leviticus and Deuteronomy amply specify what can and cannot be consumed. So again, do you want to follow the traditions of men, or yield to the Word of YHWH? What makes us think that eating swine today is okay, when the Bible is clear that it was NOT okay for the last several thousand years? When did God change His mind?

# Appendix 4

## About Christmas and Easter

Netzarim/Messianic Jewish believers adhere to the celebration of the God-ordained Biblical feasts because, unlike man-made holidays such as Christmas and Easter, the Biblical feasts are all about YHWH/Yeshua instead of "me"! They're not about spending money we don't have or going into debt to buy things we can't afford. Nobody commits suicide during the Biblical feasts because they're "feeling lonely or depressed."

### Let's begin with Christmas:

Christmas is not mentioned in the Bible; nor is there any command to celebrate the birth of our Messiah. This "holy day" was a total fabrication by man. Here are the facts:

- YHWH never said to honor His Son's birthday.

- While it's true that "Christmas" is very much ingrained into the minds of Christians who desire to honor the birth of our Savior, the fact remains, Yeshua was not born in December. By examining the Biblical feasts and reading the Scriptures in context, one can determine that He was born sometime in the September/October timeframe during the feast of Sukkot (Tabernacles), when He came to "tabernacle" among us.

- Christmas, for the most part, has become commercial to the point where Yeshua HaMashiyach (Jesus Christ) is hardly mentioned anymore, and our efforts are mainly concentrated on gift giving and money spending. Some Christians say that Christmas has been instrumental in "getting the Word out" because it witnesses to the secular world. While this might be historically true to a certain extent, this holiday is also based on several lies, including the fact that we try our best to make our children believe "Santa Claus" is real. Exactly what does "Santa" have to do with the birth of our Savior? Some say he represents the "spirit of giving" but the problem is: "Santa" has become a central figure of Christmas, taking the focus completely off Messiah! The Ninth Commandment is: "Thou shalt not lie." Lying is lying, no matter how we package it, so why would God be pleased with a deliberate yearly perpetuation of the lie of "Santa"? Some argue they've told their children there is no Santa Claus, and that their families concentrate on "the real reason for the season"– but yet, if Yeshua wasn't born on December 25th, then whose birthday are Christians celebrating?

- Except for those who realize the supposed "reason for the season" Christmas is a holiday that doesn't include Yeshua at all – which automatically makes it a lie. Most atheists, Satanists and all kinds of secular people "celebrate" Christmas, just because it's "that time of the year"– never bothering to realize that without Christ, there is no purpose for this "holiday"! Christmas to the unbeliever is a holiday to throw parties, get a day off work, get together with family and friends, and exchange presents that – if truth be told – probably shouldn't have been bought in the first place because many people end up going deeply into debt to buy gifts they can ill afford. Go to a search engine and search on something to the effect of, "What is Christmas really about?" and you will find sites that talk about everything from what people want for Christmas, to how the warm weather

> detracts from the "feel" of the holidays.
> You'll have to search long and hard to
> find the mention of Messiah......

Man has not only decided to force a December birthday on our Savior, but also to shove paganism down His throat via the use of "Christmas trees". Realizing there is symbolism and tradition behind Christmas trees, it does not detract from the fact that bringing trees into the home and decorating them was a pagan custom practiced in various parts of the world. Diligent research on this subject will reveal that trees were used as pagan altars where offerings were placed for the deity Asherah; wreaths symbolized wombs, trees symbolized phalluses, tinsel symbolized semen, and balls symbolized testes which were used to observe the sexual aspects of these pagan rituals.

Jeremiah 10 reveals how useless our man-made customs and idols are:

*Jeremiah 10: 1 Hear the word Adonai speaks to you, house of Isra'el! 2 Here is what Adonai says: "Don't learn the way of the Goyim, don't be frightened by astrological signs, even if the Goyim are afraid of them; 3 for the customs of the peoples are nothing. They cut down a tree in the forest; a craftsman works it with his axe; 4 they deck it with silver and gold. They fix it with hammer and nails, so that it won't move. 5 Like a scarecrow in a cucumber patch, it cannot speak. It has to be carried, because it cannot walk. Do not be afraid of it - it can do nothing bad; likewise, it is unable to do anything good!"*

While the above scripture doesn't specifically refer to "Christmas trees" per se, we need to remember that YHWH used to put people to death for any hint of disobedience in their worship. Leviticus 10 calls it "strange" or "unauthorized fire":

*Leviticus 10: 1 But Nadav and Avihu, sons of Aharon, each took his censer, put fire in it, laid incense on it, and offered unauthorized fire before Adonai, something he had not ordered them to do. 2 At this, fire came forth from the presence of Adonai and consumed them, so that they died in the presence of Adonai.*

If nothing else sinks in, please ask yourself this: If your birthday is on February 8th, would you want your friends and family to celebrate it on May 5th? Of course not! The same thing holds true for our Savior. He wasn't born on December 25th, so why are we celebrating His birthday then? And, in all honesty, why are we celebrating it at all, when YHWH never commanded us to?

## What about Easter?

*Ezekiel 8: 15 He said to me, "Do you see this, son of man? Yet you will see still greater abominations than these."16 Then He brought me into the inner court of the LORD'S house. And behold, at the entrance to the temple of the LORD, between the porch and the altar, were about twenty-five men with their backs to the temple of the LORD and their faces toward the east; and they were prostrating themselves eastward toward the sun. 17 He said to me, "Do you see this, son of man? Is it too light a thing for the house of Judah to commit the abominations which they have committed here, that they have filled the land with violence and provoked Me repeatedly? For behold, they are putting the twig to their nose. 18 "Therefore, I indeed will deal in wrath. My eye will have no pity nor will I spare; (NASB)*

Doesn't the above Scripture perfectly describe Easter Sunrise services? Yet this is what millions of Christians do every Easter Sunday morning! Enthralled, they stand there adoring the sun as it rises in the east, and most don't even think about the fact that they are performing the rituals of a mythical goddess called Ishtar or Astarte (Easter), or that this act resembles the ancient sun-worship of the Sun-god BAAL!

The word "Easter" is not mentioned in any Bible version except for one time in the King James – in Acts 12:4, where it was obviously mistranslated because Easter is not one of YHWH's appointed times:

*Acts 12: 4And when he had apprehended him, he put him in prison, and delivered him to four quaternions of soldiers to keep him; intending after Easter to bring him forth to the people.*

The thing is, early believers kept Passover, not Easter! Easter is simply another name for a pagan goddess and wasn't even considered a "Christian" festival until the Fourth Century.

Let's read Acts 12:4 from the Netzari Aramaic English Interlinear, translated directly from Aramaic into English:

*Acts 12:4. And he seized him and placed him in prison, and delivered him [to] sixteen soldiers to watch him so that after the Passover he might deliver him to the people of the Yehudeans.*

Passover or Pesach was originally observed by Jewish and Elohim fearing Gentiles who followed Yeshua as one body. According to letters by Jerome, Polycarp a disciple of Shaliach Yochanan (John) went to Rome in 147 AD to plead with "the church" to NOT bring Ishtar (Easter) into Christianity. Polycarp was burned at the stake for his efforts. Christians who celebrate Easter rather than Pesach and paint Easter eggs are contributing to the advancement of Paganism within the false church system. Plus, realistically, bunnies don't lay eggs....

Author Andrew Gabriel Roth on Easter:

"Easter" is mentioned in the King James, but let's take a closer look at their choice for mentioning this "holiday," which is derived from the Greek *paskha*. Here is how the world famous *Strong's Exhaustive Concordance* for King James defines this word:

> *Pas'-khah* - Noun Neuter . Definition: The paschal sacrifice (which was accustomed to be offered for the people's deliverance of old from Egypt) the paschal lamb, i.e. the lamb the Israelites were accustomed to slay and eat on the fourteenth day of the month of Nisan (the first month of their year) in memory of

the day on which their fathers, preparing to depart from Egypt, were bidden by God to slay and eat a lamb, and to sprinkle their door posts with its blood, that the destroying angel, seeing the blood, might pass over their dwellings; Christ crucified is likened to the slain paschal lamb the paschal supper the paschal feast, the feast of the Passover, extending from the 14th to the 20th day of the month Nisan.

King James Word Usage - Total: 29
Passover 28, Easter 1

Please note the last line. Twenty-eight times in the New Testament *paskha* is understood to mean Passover. There is a good reason for this: It is the same exact word for Passover from the Greek, the Hebrew original being *pesach*. Notice also that Strong's is trying to suggest the Passover is likened to the sacrifice of Y'shua, but they don't come right out and justify calling it "Easter" because in every other place the meaning is absolute and incontrovertible. Nor do they offer any explanation for the variant reading of "Easter" in Acts 12:4. So now, according to the New International Version, here are the 29 occurrences of *paskha*:

*"As you know, the **Passover** (paskha) is two days away--and the Son of Man will be handed over to be crucified."...On the first day of the Feast of Unleavened Bread, the disciples came to Jesus and asked, "Where do you want us to make preparations for you to eat the **Passover** (paskha)?" He replied,*

*"Go into the city to a certain man and tell him, 'The Teacher says: My appointed time is near. I am going to celebrate the **Passover** (paskha) with my disciples at your house.'" So the disciples did as Jesus had directed them and prepared the **Passover** (paskha). (Matthew 26:2, 17-19)*

*Now the **Passover** (paskha) and the Feast of Unleavened Bread were only two days away, and the chief priests and the teachers of the law were looking for some sly way to arrest Jesus and kill him...On the first day of the Feast of Unleavened Bread, when it was customary to sacrifice the **Passover** (paskha) lamb, Jesus' disciples asked him, "Where do you want us to go and make preparations for you to eat the Passover?"...Say to the owner of the house he enters, 'The Teacher asks: Where is my guest room, where I may eat the **Passover** (paskha) with my disciples?'...The disciples left, went into the city and found things just as Jesus had told them. So they prepared the **Passover** (paskha). (Mark 14:1, 12, 14, 16)*

*Every year his parents went to Jerusalem for the Feast of the **Passover** (paskha). (Luke 2:41)*

*Now the Feast of Unleavened Bread, called the **Passover** (paskha), was approaching...Then came the day of Unleavened Bread on which the **Passover** (paskha) lamb had to be sacrificed, Jesus sent Peter and John, saying, "Go and make preparations for us to eat the Passover."...And say to the owner of the house, 'The Teacher asks: Where is the guest room, where I may eat the **Passover** (paskha) with my disciples?'...They left and found things just as Jesus had told them. So they prepared the **Passover** (paskha)...And he said to them, "I have eagerly desired to eat this **Passover** (paskha) with you before I suffer. (Luke 22:1, 7-8, 11,13, 15)*

*When it was almost time for the Jewish* **Passover** *(paskha), Jesus went up to Jerusalem.  (John 2:13)*

*Now while he was in Jerusalem at the* **Passover** *(paskha) Feast, many people saw the miraculous signs he was doing and believed in his name.*
*(John 2:23)*

*When he arrived in Galilee, the Galileans welcomed him. They had seen all that he had done in Jerusalem at the* **Passover** *(paskha) Feast, for they also had been there.  (John 4:45)*

*The Jewish* **Passover** *(paskha) Feast was near.  (John 6:4)*

*When it was almost time for the Jewish* **Passover** *(paskha), many went up from the country to Jerusalem for their ceremonial cleansing before the* **Passover** *(paskha).  (John 11:55)*

*Six days before the* **Passover** *(paskha), Jesus arrived at Bethany, where Lazarus lived, whom Jesus had raised from the dead.  (John 12:1)*

*It was just before the* **Passover** *(paskha) Feast. Jesus knew that the time had come for him to leave this world and go to the Father. Having loved his own who were in the world, he now showed them the full extent of his love.  (John 13:1)*

*Then the Jews led Jesus from Caiaphas to the palace of the Roman governor. By now it was early morning, and to avoid ceremonial uncleanness the Jews did not enter the palace; they wanted to be able to eat the* **Passover** *(paskha).  (John 18:28)*

*But it is your custom for me to release to you one prisoner at the time of the **Passover** (paskha). Do you want me to release 'the king of the Jews'?" (John 18:39)*

*It was the day of Preparation of **Passover** (paskha) Week, about the sixth hour. "Here is your king," Pilate said to the Jews. (John 19:14)*

*After arresting him, he put him in prison, handing him over to be guarded by four squads of four soldiers each. Herod intended to bring him out for public trial after the **Passover** (paskha). (Acts 12:4)*

(Pesach [Passover] also makes sense because even if "Easter" did exist as a holiday it could hardly be termed a security threat that Herod had to worry about! What threat did the term "Easter" pose to the Jewish festival commemorating FREEDOM FROM A FOREIGN POWER that forced Rome to take extra measures to prevent riots in the first place? Why else would Pilate in the Gospels offer to free a prisoner if not to placate this volatile situation?)

*Get rid of the old yeast that you may be a new batch without yeast--as you really are. For Christ, our **Passover** (paskha) lamb, has been sacrificed. (1 Corinthians 5:7)*

*By faith he kept the **Passover** (paskha) and the sprinkling of blood, so that the destroyer of the firstborn would not touch the firstborn of Israel. (Hebrews 11:28)*

Notice that the NIV also renders Acts 12:4 as Passover. In fact, the KJV is alone in this kind of scholarly dishonesty, as the root and usage of *paskha/pesach* could not be clearer.

As you can see, there is an Easter Festival of sorts that is mentioned in the Bible, but it seems it is not the kind of holiday the righteous were supposed to attend! Seeing also the consistent linkage of Asherah with poles, trees and groves, a very similar "sacred" occasion mentioned in Tanakh has also ironically been co-opted by another Christian holiday:

*Hear what YHWH says to you, O house of Israel. This is what YHWH says: "Do not learn the ways of the nations or be terrified by signs in the sky, though the nations are terrified by them. For the customs of the peoples are worthless; they cut a tree out of the forest, and a craftsman shapes it with his chisel. They adorn it with silver and gold; they fasten it with hammer and nails so it will not totter. Like a scarecrow in a melon patch, their idols cannot speak; they must be carried because they cannot walk. Do not fear them; they can do no harm nor can they do any good." No one is like you, O YHWH; you are great, and your name is mighty in power. Who should not revere you, O King of the nations? This is your due. Among all the wise men of the nations and in all their kingdoms, there is no one like you. They are all senseless and foolish; they are taught by worthless wooden idols. Hammered silver is brought from Tarshish and gold from Uphaz. What the craftsman and goldsmith have made is then dressed in blue and purple-- all made by skilled workers. But YHWH is the true Elohim; he is the living Elohim, the eternal King. When he is angry, the earth trembles; the nations cannot endure his wrath. "Tell them this: 'These gods, who did not make the heavens and the earth, will perish from the earth and from under the heavens.'" (Jeremiah 10:1-11)*

Additionally, we should remember that Asherah/ Astarte/Eostre/Ester derived power ultimately from her male counterpart Baal who, not be outdone, had a biblical "holiday" of his own under his other title, Molech. He even had a "sponsor" from one of the most famous people in biblical history:

*As Solomon grew old, his wives turned his heart after other gods, and his heart was not fully devoted to YHWH his Elohim, as the heart of David his father had been. He followed Ashtoreth the goddess of the Sidonians, and Molech the detestable god of the Ammonites. So Solomon did evil in the eyes of YHWH ; he did not follow YHWH completely, as David his father had done. On a hill east of Jerusalem, Solomon built a high place for Chemosh the detestable god of Moab, and for Molech the detestable god of the Ammonites. He did the same for all his foreign wives, who burned incense and offered sacrifices to their gods. (1 Kings 11:4-8)*

And exactly what kind of festival took place in honor of the "old time religion"?

*He also tore down the quarters of the male shrine prostitutes, which were in the temple of YHWH and where women did weaving for Asherah. Josiah brought all the priests from the towns of Judah and desecrated the high places, from Geba to Beersheba, where the priests had burned incense. He broke down the shrines at the gates--at the entrance to the Gate of Joshua, the city governor, which is on the left of the city gate. Although the priests of the high places did not serve at the altar of YHWH in Jerusalem, they ate unleavened bread with their fellow priests. He desecrated Topheth, which was in the Valley of Ben Hinnom, so no one could use it to sacrifice his son or daughter in the fire to Molech.*

Judges 10:6-15 outlines how the anger of ADONAI blazed against Isra'el because they served foreign and pagan gods. Has anything changed that would cause Him to rejoice in our pagan worship today? If not, then why continue with the false teachings of Christmas and Easter?

The bottom line is, Yeshua didn't rise on "Easter" - He died on Nisan 14 (which falls on different days from our Gregorian calendar filled with the names of weeks and months of pagan deities), and rose exactly three days later. YHWH made a huge deal out of letting us know that Passover is ALWAYS on Nisan 14 and that the Resurrection was exactly three days later. Why would He be happy with us changing the day and calling it "Easter" after a pagan goddess?

# Appendix 5

## YHWH's calendar and the seven-day week

How do we know that Saturday is the seventh day? Let's check it out:

YHWH said in Genesis that the sky is useful.

*Genesis 1: 14 God said, 'Let there be lights in the dome of the sky to divide the day from the night; let them be for signs, seasons, days and years; and let them be for lights in the dome of the sky to give light on the earth'; and that is how it was".*

This He did on the 4th day of the creation. The fourth Day? Yes the 4th day - Man was not created till the 6th day. So we can safely say that the calendar, the mechanism for determining seasons, days, and years has ALWAYS existed, since it existed before man. It was a gift of God. A gift to the man he had not yet even created.

Now look at Genesis 3:17. *"To Adam he said, 'Because you listened to what your wife said and ate from the tree about which I gave you the order, 'You are not to eat from it,' the ground is cursed on your account; you will work hard to eat from it as long as you live. 18 It will produce thorns and thistles for you, and you will eat field plants. 19 'You will eat bread by the sweat of your forehead till you return to the ground -....'"*

And, verse 24: *"So he drove the man out...."* that is, out of the garden and into the unprepared fields.

Now, Chapter 5 verse 5: *In all, Adam lived 930 years, and then he died.*

ADONAI does not tell us what Adam did during his life for the whole 930 years, nor does the Bible tell us if God simply told Adam everything he needed to know or if He required Adam to learn by trial and error - but one thing is for sure: From Chapter 3 verse 24, Adam was no longer in the lush prepared-for-him garden where all he had to do was stroll with God and work the rich land which received its water from the river (Gen 2:10). And from Chapter 3, verse 17, Adam had to work hard to eat, and that means he had to gather and plant and harvest and clear the thorns and thistles and develop agriculture.

If YHWH did not directly tell Adam what to do (and we don't know for sure whether He did or not), then Adam had to use his ingenuity and watch the stars to determine the seasons. Since he lived 930 years you can be sure after watching the stars for nearly a millennium, he KNEW how the stars reflected the seasons and how to tell when the seasons were changing and when to plant and harvest. If he got it wrong the first few seasons when he and Eve were on their own, you can bet he figured out enough afterward that he could look up at the night sky and know exactly how many weeks and days he had to prepare and sow his fields, and exactly when he needed to harvest. He had 900 or more opportunities to get it right!

Yes, Adam used the signs YHWH created on day 4 of the creation as a calendar, and it is to Adam, no doubt, we owe the 12-month year because you can be sure that Adam recognized that the moon appeared in the evening sky almost exactly 12 times before the same stars appeared in the same place in the morning sky again. In fact, you can be sure, that after 900 some-odd years of observing the night sky, Adam knew that you could not count an exact number of days between observations of a new moon. Go observe the moon for yourself for a few years, and you'll be able to draw the same conclusion....

It is interesting to note that to use this calendar of the sky it does not have to be written down. You don't need a calendar on a piece of paper to tell you it is September or March (using our modern names for the months)! You only have to note the position of the stars at sunset or sunrise and count days between the events in the sky, and the moon helped you know how many days had passed. And do you think for a moment that Adam kept this information to himself?

Hardly! He taught what he learned to his sons and daughters, and they passed it on to their offspring.

## Origin of the Week

Now let's turn for a moment back to the creation.

*Genesis 2: 2 "On the seventh day God was finished with his work which he had made, so he rested on the seventh day from all his work which he had made. 3 God blessed the seventh day and separated it as holy; because on that day God rested from all his work which he had created, so that it itself could produce."*

Here we have at least the origin of the number "seven" as important to God. Whether you accept that the "day" was a 24 hour day, or an epoch lasting a thousand years, or 10,000 years for each "day," the point is God created for 6 "days" and rested on the 7th. Then He blessed the 7th day and separated it as holy.

Now, it is plainly obvious that our seven day week came from the creation, and is so intuitively obvious there really needs be no further analysis of the origin of the 7-day week, but there are countless people out there who simply can't see this, and attempt to argue all sorts of "mystical" or pagan origins of the 7-day week so we are simply forced to study this further.

We've already been shown that God blessed the 7th day. In Genesis chapter 7, verse 4, God tells Noah that in "seven more days" he would cause it to begin to rain. In Genesis chapter 8, Noah, after waiting for the waters to recede, sent out a dove which returned to him because there was no place to land. So Noah waited another 7 days to send out the dove again (verse 10). The dove still came back, albeit with an olive branch, so Noah waited another 7 days (verse 12) before he sent the dove out again. Can anyone argue that Noah was observing a seven day period that was quite normal for him? In chapter 7, verse 4 we find YHWH Himself telling Noah that in "7 more days" he would begin the rains. Clearly, intuitively, we see that God referred to 7 days because Noah understood seven days. The seven-day period was already well established with man!

Many argue that the patriarchs did not have to obey the Sabbath, and did not have the seven day week since neither is specifically cited in Genesis. But examine Genesis for yourself. It is a book describing man's revolt against God and the consequences. It is not a book of instruction and it was not given to the patriarchs to "live by." Genesis is only a record of events, written long after their occurrence, recorded by Moses some 2,500 years after the events described in Genesis (in fact, the patriarchs were long dead by the time it was written) and it was not intended to provide the commandments. (Interestingly, the commandments – God's teaching and instruction - are not written until Moses reaches his own time in the book of Exodus.)

Genesis provides enough history to set the stage and establish the foundation on which the path to the Messiah begins. It is not a complete history book, and it is not a "history of creation." It does not describe the origins of all things human; it does not record the exact "hows" and "whys" man did what he did; and, indeed, it does not specifically identify the origin of the 7-day week nor does it clearly reveal that the Patriarchs were given the Sabbath and that they observed the Sabbath (though Adam was clearly present when God declared the seventh day holy). It simply can't include all aspects of human life at the time, and we therefore are forced to realize that some things in the behavior of man in this era were given by God, and not written down. The fact that man, very likely, always observed the seven day week is hinted at (i.e. the discussion of Noah above). That a seven day week would be observed and not include the Sabbath – the very day by which a week is defined – is an unlikely outcome.

It is quite comical the lengths to which some authors will try to "prove" that the seven day week originated in the Babylonian Empire circa 600 B.C. citing "astrology," linking the fact that there were only seven visible objects in the sky that were clearly not "fixed stars" (i.e., Sun, Moon, Mercury, Venus, Mars, Jupiter, and Saturn), and naming the days of the week after the "gods" of these planets. Curiously, these same authors don't discover that Byzantine historian Anna Comnena (1083-1153AD) said in her writings: "The art of divination is a rather recent discovery, *unknown to the ancient world* [emphasis added]. In the time of Eudoxus [c.408-355 BC], the distinguished astronomer, the rules for it did not exist, and Plato had no knowledge of the science; even Manetho the astrologer [c.280 BC] had no accurate information on the subject. In their attempts to prophesy they lacked the horoscope and the fixing of cardinal points; they did not know how to observe the position of the stars at one's nativity and all the other things that the inventor of this system has bequeathed to posterity, things intelligible to the devotees of such nonsense." [The Alexiad of Anna Comnena, translated by E.R.A. Sewter, Penguin Classics, 1969, pp.193-194]. And even more curious is that these same authors don't question the **idea** of a "seven day week" in the first place, they simply try to fit astrology and paganism into the **names** of the days of the seven day week that was already well entrenched in and observed in the ancient world! A few authors recognize there is no astronomical correlation to explain a seven day week, yet they fail to see the obvious and conclude that the pagan names of the days of the week were given to the days of a 7 day week **that already was in use**!

**Back to the Calendar**

Now let's return to the calendar. Adam could see that the moon appeared in the evening sky pretty close to 12 times, before the same stars would again appear in the same place in the evening sky. Even if Adam did not know what "12" was, that is, even if he did not understand the concept of "counting," he could put notches on a stick, or mark the walls of a cave each time he saw the moon and see that he had the "same number" of notches for the appearance of the moon each "year." But there is no doubt that he would have noticed that the 12th time he saw the moon, the stars that same night weren't quite in the same place as they were the last time he saw the moon's 12th appearance. He probably did not understand why this was so, but he probably did notice that all he had to do was to wait a few more days and the stars were back in the same place as they were the year before. That is, he may not have been able to discern the tropical year, i.e., 365.25 days.

So, whether or not Adam could count does not matter. He would have known that sometimes after observing "12" appearances of the moon, the stars would be in the same place many days later than they appeared the year before. What did Adam need to do about this? Nothing! Since he did not rely on a written calendar, the fact that the stars were "late" did not matter, he simply watched, and sure enough, a few days later, they were in the right place and he knew when to plant. The monthly appearance of the moon helped him "count" days, but the stars reappeared in the same place in the sky, like clockwork, whether or not the moon made exactly 12 appearances.

Why spend so much time describing what Adam knew about the moon and the stars? Because later in this treatise we are going to discuss the calendar in some detail and the concepts as understood by Adam will be important. But for now, let's turn back to Noah.

In Genesis 7:11, we find the following statement: *"On the seventh day of the second month of the 600th year of Noah's life...."* From this we know that God told Moses - who penned these words which became the book of Genesis - that in Noah's time, a definite calendar existed, complete with identified months and specific days. Here we have evidence that a complete calendar existed in Noah's time.

Realizing also that Adam must have known the concept of a "month," and that he also understood there was not an exact, integral relationship between the appearance of the moon and the number of days in a year, then in the intervening centuries between Adam and Noah, there was much development in the establishment of a calendar! It would not be a stretch to conclude that by the time of Noah, Adam and his descendants had established enough observation and refinement that the calendar had been written down, and Noah was certainly aware of how to use it! Notice that Moses, in Genesis, did not need to spend time describing what a "month" was, nor how many days were in each month, nor how it came about. The calendar was already as common as eating, drinking, sleeping, and any other human activity!

Now let us go to the time of the Babylonian Empire, around 600 BC. Note that Moses lived around 1500 to 1400 BC, and though Moses did not describe the calendar, early societies just before the Babylonians certainly did. We see in these ancient societies attempts to bring the lunar year (about 354 days) into line with the solar (agricultural) year of approximately 365 days. They did this by crudely adding months to the year when they thought they were needed to maintain a division of the year into two seasons, basically summer, and winter.

Given that the moon did not make exactly 12 appearances in a year, then the calendar, (which was quite naturally based on the moon in that age of man), would get "out of sync" with the sun, which completed a "year" some 11 days later than the period of time the moon completed 12 "appearances" or "months." The beginning of summer for example would "drift" into another month, and it became impossible to figure out when to plant! To account for this changing summer, they had to make the lunar calendar "sync up" once again with the "solar" calendar by adding extra months! The details of this are beyond the scope of this text but it is an interesting study in itself, and you are encouraged dig into it.

Babylon is of interest because they used a calendar of months based on a curious observation of the moon. They knew that the appearance of the moon, compared to the background of stars, not only made monthly reappearances which they fit into months of 29 or 30 days, but the moon also made an interesting repeated, long-term cycle. That repeated long-term cycle was that the moon made almost exactly 235 "appearances" before it once again "appeared" in front of exactly the same group of stars on the same day the sun was back, once again, in the same place relative to its annual cycle.

This cycle of 235 lunar appearances happened in "exactly" 19 years. This cycle, even today is still called the "Metonic cycle" named after the Greek philosopher, Meton, of Athens, around 440 B.C. who first understood the mathematics behind the 19 year cycle of the moon. The 19 year cycle is off by only 0.09 days, or two hours, which is why the word "exactly" is in quotes above. It is not astronomically "exact," but to ancient man, without modern time keeping, it is phenomenally "exact." Suffice it to say that the Babylonians added an extra "month" to a year every once in a while making some years contain 13 months, the same as their ancestors, but on a well-prescribed plan. The years with 13 months were the 3rd, 6th, 8th, 11th, 14th, 17th, and 19th of the 19 year lunar cycle! This is an even mathematical distribution, which, interestingly, adds 7 months every 19 years, and keeps the lunar and solar calendars in sync!

Now, back to our discussion of Adam. Adam made observations of the moon, no doubt. Adam had to plant and reap, no doubt. Adam had to understand the seasons, and when to plant and reap. Adam passed this knowledge to his offspring, no doubt. His offspring continued to observe the moon, sun, and stars and refine the observations, no doubt. Mankind continued to refine these observations, no doubt. Now, when the Babylonians began to establish their society, some 3,400 years after Adam, there seems no doubt that much of what the Babylonians knew about the lunar and solar calendar was already very well known!

Case in point: The beginning of the month in the Babylonian calendar was determined by the direct observation of the "young" crescent moon at sunset when it was known the moon would reappear as a "new moon." This custom, clearly taken from the ancient Israelites, is in line with the idea that the new day begins at sunset, as originated in Genesis.

Now the scoffer reading this text might say, "But I don't believe in Adam, so I don't buy what you are saying." It doesn't matter if you believe in Adam or not. It is well documented in many historical writings and manuscripts from the period around 1450 B.C. that refer to Moses as a real person, and all these calendar observations are from his time which still precede Babylon by a 1000 years! Babylon simply used/modified the concept of a calendar already established in society! Babylon eventually fell and Rome took over and the calendar continued to be modified to suit the empire of the moment. More about this in the following paragraphs.

### Significance of "7 days"

The Babylonian calendar, even though it kept the moon and the sun "in sync," had problems. It seems the seasons drifted by days over hundreds of years. By the time the Roman Empire was in control, the seasons were still seriously messed up. Julius Caesar attempted to fix the problem of the seasonal drift by creating a new calendar.

In the year 46 BC, Julius Caesar reformed the Roman calendar to what he hoped would be a more manageable form. By this time, astronomers understood the solar year was really not astronomically connected to the moon, so Julius changed the number of days in the months to achieve a 365 day year and separated the solar calendar from the lunar calendar. To "catch up" with the seasons, Julius Caesar also added 90 days to the year 46 BC between November and February.

Before we go on, another interesting study is the influence Emperors and Rulers have had on the calendar. In 8 BC, emperor Augustus renamed the 6th month of the Roman calendar from "Sextilus" to "August." Julius Caesar in 44 B.C. renamed the 5th month from "Quintilis" to "July." In 45 B.C., Julius Caesar made 1 January the start of the year.

However, the church didn't like the wild parties that took place at the start of the new year, and in AD 567 declared that having the year start on January 1st was an "ancient mistake" that should be abolished. Various New Year dates were used; there are at least seven documented periods where the start of the new year was changed to March 1st, January 1st, March 25th, December 25th, or the Saturday before Easter, or some variation. The Byzantine Empire used a year starting on 1 September.

Continuing, the Julian calendar consisted of cycles of three 365-day years followed by a 366-day "leap" the fourth year. Around 9 B.C., it was determined that the priests in charge of computing the calendar had been adding leap years every three years instead of four!

Consequently, to correct the error, no leap years were added from 9 B.C. to 8 A.D. Leap years were therefore 45 BC, 42 BC, 39 BC, 36 BC, 33 BC, 30 BC, 27 BC, 24 BC, 21 BC, 18 BC, 15 BC, 12 BC, 9 BC, 8 AD, 12 AD, and every fourth year thereafter.

The details of the calendar and its changes and problems are extraordinarily interesting, but this text is already quite long so recognizing that the Julian calendar introduces an error of 1 day every 128 years, by the mid 1500's A.D., the Julian calendar was off "season" by 10 days and the calendar, once again, needed to be corrected. The "Gregorian" calendar proposed by Aloysius Lilius, a physician from Naples, was adopted by Pope Gregory XIII to correct the errors of the Julian Calendar.

It was decreed by Pope Gregory XIII in a "papal bull" (a charter bearing an official seal) on 24 February 1582. By the stroke of a pen, 4 October 1582 was followed by 15 October 1582. This corrected the 10 days accumulated error of the Julian Calendar, and established a far more accurate handling of "leap years," so that it takes about 3,300 years to accumulate an error of 1 day (compared to the 1 day error every 128 in the Julian calendar).

The careful reader will make note of the following: Considering all of the above, the development of and changes to the calendar; the addition of months; the addition or subtraction of days due to calendar errors; the addition of "leap years"; the complete change from one calendar to another; changes to the beginning of the year; and many other changes noted in the historical record leads to one inescapable discovery: There is no historical record suggesting the steady, 7-day week, has ever been broken! When Julius Caesar added his 90 days to correct for errors in the Babylonian/Roman calendar, the date changed, not the day of the week. When the Gregorian calendar came into effect in 1582, the date changed, not the day of the week. Considering the supreme power emperors, kings, and rulers have had over the millennia, none have changed the day of the week. Since at least the days of Moses, the 7-day cycle has run completely uninterrupted – whether we call it a "week" or call the days Saturday, Sunday, Monday, etc, or simply day 1, 2, 3, etc., it has been that way as far back as mankind has records!

We have seen in this appendix, that Noah was well familiar with the 7-day period (whether or not it was called a "week"), such that it was his chosen period to wait for sending out a bird to determine if the flood waters had receded. So there is evidence that the seven day week has progressed unbroken since the time of Noah, and since the lives of Adam, and Lamech, the father of Noah, overlapped and Lamech lived till Shem (son of Noah) was 93 years old, the 7-day week was most certainly passed from generation to generation from Adam to the present day! If you don't find that fascinating, and if you don't find something quite substantial in this, you need to re-read this section till it sinks in!

The seven day week has never been broken!

As far as we can tell from all available historical records, the earliest accounting for days was simply numbered. The seventh day was the last day of the cycle, and was the Sabbath set aside for God. Despite a long history since the resurrection of the Messiah where the "Christian Church" has foolishly attempted to change the day of rest to the first day, Sunday, the seven day cycle still has not been broken. Those who wish to obey God, Exodus 20:10-11, and observe the Sabbath and keep it holy may be comforted to know that if you can determine the number of years which have passed since Adam, and divide the number of total days since then by 7, you will know exactly the number of weeks that have passed and know that the Sabbath you are observing is the same Sabbath observed since the beginning!

The fact is that since the dawn of man, by the hand of YHVH, the seven day period was established, the 7th day declared "set aside" and "holy," a day of rest – and despite the many opportunities by man to alter it (even still today), it has never been altered!

# Appendix 6

## Questions for Mainstream Christians who cannot let go of the "Jesus nailed it to the cross" idea

**Question:** Was Jesus a Jew or a Gentile? (Don't laugh - many Christians don't know the answer to this!)

**Answer:** Yeshua was a Torah observant, tallit wearing, synagogue attending, Sabbath and feast-keeping, kosher Jew. Are today's Christians, for the most part, walking in Torah, keeping the Biblical feasts, or the seventh day Sabbath? Various sects of Catholicism and many Christian denominations claim to be the "true religion" that Jesus established, yet, modern day Christianity has very little in common with the Founder of their "faith"!

**Question:** Why do Christians refer to the Jewish Messiah as "Jesus" when Yeshua was His given Hebrew name? It's not that hard to pronounce....

181

**Answer:** Our Jewish Messiah's given name is pronounced "Yeshua". This is a transliteration of the Hebrew יֵשׁוּעַ spelled in various ways including Yahshua, Y'Shua, etc. "Jesus" is the Hellenized-Anglicized form of "Yeshua". The name Jesus doesn't mean anything, while Yeshua means "YHWH Saves" or "YHWH is Salvation".[5] Yeshua never heard the name "Jesus" in His lifetime. Some people have said that this is irrelevant, but the question is this: If your name is John or Mary, why would you answer to Charles or Betty? Probably not, because that isn't your name! Yes, Yeshua knows who we are talking about when we call Him "Jesus", but it's a lot more rewarding to call Him by His given Name – the Name that has an important meaning.

**Question:** Who will enter the gates of the New Jerusalem?

---

5 The Tanakh records the name Y'shua (Jeshua) 30 times, Y'hoshua (Joshua) 199 times. Y'shua is the shortened form of Y'hoshua, the same name given to Mashiyach. The successor of Moses, Y'hoshua (Joshua), is a type of Mashiyach who brought the Israelites into the promised land. Additionally, yeshua (salvation) used 78 times is the passive participle of yasha (save or savior), which is used 205 times. "I have waited for your yeshua (salvation), O YHWH." Genesis 49:18. The hybrid name Jesus (Je-Zeus) was coined within a culture where "Zeus" is the chief deity. The name "Jesus" contributes to the polytheistic values that breaks Mashiyach away from his Torah based identity. The Greek persona of the "new Messiah" made way to endorse Trinitarian, anti-Torah and Hellenistic lifestyles. (Roth's Netzari Aramaic English Interlinear)

**Answer:** The 12 tribes of Isra'el. Not Christians, Muslims, Hindus or the Ku Klux Klan; only the 12 tribes of Isra'el (Revelation 21:12). And who is ISRAEL? All believers in Messiah Yeshua!

**Question:** Where in the Scriptures does YHWH tell us to ignore the seventh day Sabbath – the day He Himself blessed and made holy (Genesis 2:1-2)? (Please don't insist that the Sabbath was changed to Sunday because "Jesus rose on a Sunday" as this is not true, as shown earlier in this book....)

**Answer:** Throughout the Bible one can find absolutely no evidence that YHWH or Yeshua ever claimed the first day or placed any special blessing upon it. Furthermore, you won't find anything in the Scriptures that references the changing of the Sabbath to Sunday. Some argue that Constantine was responsible for changing the Sabbath because he hated the Jews. Regardless, in Yeshua's time, both Jews and Gentiles alike attended the synagogues on the seventh day as evidenced in Acts 13:42-44 which shows that the early Gentile believers were Torah observant, in part, because they requested further instruction of Paul "on the next Sabbath" (Saturday/the seventh day). We're told almost the whole city arrived for the meeting on the "next Sabbath" and that no separate Sunday (first day) "sabbaths" were being held by anyone.

**Question:** Christians insist that "the law" was abolished. How is that possible when sin is transgression of "the law"? When and by whom was it abolished? Certainly not by Yeshua! He said He came **not** to abolish but to confirm. Why would Yeshua's role as "Final Sin Sacrifice" in any way negate Torah – God's original teaching and instruction? Christians insist that "the law" was "written on our hearts" (Jeremiah 31:33-34; Romans 10:4-8) and therefore, those old, outdated "OT" commands no longer pertain to them. How can you know what "the law" is, if you don't first study and learn to obey it? Man is born into sin; he does not automatically know "right" from "wrong"- which is what Torah is all about; it's our divine blueprint for moral behavior.

**Answer:** Yeshua is our "New Covenant" and "Final Sin Sacrifice" who was YHWH in the Flesh. YHWH gave us a New **Covenant**, not a new Torah! Please also note, He did not make a "new covenant" with the Gentiles, but with Houses of Judah and Isra'el who were and still are Torah observant because that is what YHWH commanded of His People.

Yeshua's blood sacrifice covers only unintentional/ inadvertent sins that were committed in ignorance (Hebrews 9:7). Sins against Torah (which you are supposed to know and **obey** since it is "written on our hearts" – Jeremiah 31:32, Deuteronomy 11:18, 2 Corinthians 3:2-3) are **not** covered! This is why Paul spent so much time in Hebrews explaining the meaning of Yeshua's death. The sacrifice of the Messiah was for your **unintentional** sins; not continued, deliberate sins. "Mercy" and "Grace" do NOT invalidate Torah!

**Question:** In 1 Corinthians 5:7-8, what Feast did Paul tell us to observe?

**Answer:** Passover - not "Easter" with its paganistic roots. Passover has always been on Nisan 14 since the time Moses helped the Israelites escape from Pharoah. It doesn't fall on the day Christians celebrate Easter! Yeshua died on Passover and rose exactly three days later on the Sabbath. Easter and Passover have nothing whatsoever in common – not to mention that "Easter" was the name of a pagan deity, so why would YHWH honor our celebration of Easter? Has He ever been happy about paganism?

**Question:** In view of the fact that YHWH said to celebrate the Biblical feasts forever (Leviticus 23:21, 31, 41, Exodus 12:14), why do you believe He wants you to ignore them now, simply because His Son died on the cross? Has "forever" come and gone, or somehow ended? If so, then please explain why Yeshua has so far only fulfilled FOUR of the seven Biblical Feasts – and the next one to be fulfilled is what Christians term the "rapture"....

**Answer:** Yeshua has fulfilled the first four of the seven Biblical feasts, which logically means He will fulfill the last three, as well. Since the first four feasts have already been fulfilled, the next one to be fulfilled is Rosh Hashana – the Feast of Trumpets: the so-called "Rapture" (which, by the way, does not allow "the church" to be zapped out of here before the Great Tribulation, as many Christians seem to think – but that's a whole new topic in itself).

Believers in Messiah are to celebrate the Biblical feasts because it is instructed by God in the Torah for Isra'el to observe these festivals **forever** (Leviticus 23:21, 31, 41, Exodus 12:14). (Remember, as believers in the Jewish Messiah, YOU are part of Isra'el...) Our Savior observed these festivals as did the early "Messianic Jews" and apostles such as Rabbi Shaul/Apostle Paul (Acts 20:16, 1 Corinthians 16:8, Acts 28:17). When Yeshua returns to Earth these festivals will be re-established worldwide (Zechariah 14:16-21). YHWH has His appointed times! He does nothing without purpose. What makes us think we can simply ignore what He says?

**Question:** Did Rav Sha'ul (Apostle Paul) actually say that, since Yeshua's death, we can eat whatever we want, meaning there is no more "kosher"?

**Answer:** When read in context, the answer is a resounding "No!" Kosher Law always was, and still is, God's Law. YHWH never said pork, shellfish, etc. were food! People called these things food in rebellion against Him. The passages in question within the "New Testament" deal with animals God gave us to eat and whether they are ceremonially clean and can be eaten at that time. Even in Peter's vision (Acts 11), Peter knew which animals he could not eat because he observed Torah. The vision was illustrating that the Gentiles were now to be accepted!

The rest of the passage in Acts 11 shows that this is the correct interpretation and what the vision was all about.

**Question:** If the Torah was "abolished" and the "Old Testament" is to be ignored, why are Christians still teaching the Ten Commandments or telling church members to tithe? Have you ever thought to ask your pastor why you have to tithe 10 percent from what is referred to as the "Old Testament", and yet not keep the seventh day Sabbath or the Biblical Feasts? Isn't it hypocritical to pick and choose?

**Answer:** You won't find anything in the Scriptures to show that Torah was ever abolished. Many Christians have decided that when God said, *"I will put my laws in their minds and write them on their hearts,"* He meant that His original Torah (teachings) would be rendered null and void. How many people today automatically know God's laws? How many actually **obey** his laws? If it were truly the case that God's laws were somehow imprinted in our hearts, there would be NO cases of adultery, divorce, murder, hate crimes, abortion, lying, stealing, coveting – things that many Christians, too, are guilty of....Torah being written on our hearts means that knowing Torah, we would want to obey and follow.

Yeshua said: *Matthew 5: 17 Don't think that I have come to abolish the Torah or the Prophets. I have come not to abolish but to complete. 18 Yes indeed! I tell you that until heaven and earth pass away, not so much as a yud or a stroke*

187

*will pass from the Torah - not until everything that must happen has happened.*

If "ALL" hasn't happened yet, and heaven and earth have not passed away, then what makes us think we can do as we please? Let's take Matthew 5 a little further while we're in the vicinity:

*Matthew 5: 20 For I say to you that unless your righteousness exceeds more than that of the scribes and the Pharisees,*

Yeshua would certainly not mention "the Pharisees" in this context, except that they walked in a degree of righteousness. Most ancient and modern Pharisees (Orthodox) have disciplined and righteous lifestyles; therefore Yeshua is stating the difference. As the Ruach haKodesh writes Torah upon the hearts of his followers, they will surpass the righteousness of the Pharisees who elevate tradition rather than Torah. Those without Torah have NO righteousness, and they are certainly not "borrowing" any from Mashiyach's righteousness while they continue in sin, regardless of what their theologians have to say. Mashiyach imparts his righteousness to those who follow him, and keep Torah. Through Yeshua, YHWH is raising up a Set Apart people who Keep His Commandments rather than their own religious traditions.

**Question:** Do the Scriptures command us to celebrate the birth or resurrection of the Messiah via the man-made "holy days" of Christmas and Easter? What's more, is it okay to lie to your children about the existence of Santa Claus and egg-laying rabbits?

What do these things have to do with Yeshua's birth and death? For those who want to answer: "It's fun; it's tradition" or even, "my kids know there's no Santa Claus or Easter bunny and our family knows the real reason for the season" then please check the Bible to see what God says about man-made traditions.

**Answer:** You simply won't find Christmas and Easter anywhere in the Bible. Those holidays were man's idea and Satan encouraged us to insert paganistic traditions to lead us away from the Truth. What's more, it is simply not okay to lie to your children about the existence of Santa Claus and egg-laying rabbits. Lying is a sin that breaks the Ninth Commandment. Can you honestly say that you've never said to your kids: "Santa Claus is coming soon to bring you toys, so you'd better be good!" or "Look! The Easter bunny brought you some colored eggs!" Is it okay to tell a "little" lie? Since when? Is human tradition worth the cost of making us guilty of sinning in God's eyes?

**Question:** How many denominations comprise the body of Yeshua, according to Scripture?

**Answer:** There are no "denominations" in YHWH's Kingdom! **All** believers are "the seed of Abraham" and therefore, part of Israel (Galatians 3:29).

**Question:** Do you realize that the original followers of Yeshua and His disciples were all Torah observant? Do you realize that Christianity was borne out of

Catholicism which had totally twisted the teachings of Yeshua? That being the case, how can today's Christians claim that their respective churches are the "original church that Jesus built" when none of them observe Torah, and most of them ignore the seventh day Sabbath and the Biblical feasts? Does your church in any way resemble anything that Yeshua originally taught? Please check the Bible thoroughly before answering.

**Answer:** Throughout the Tanakh, Gentiles were considered to be immoral heathens and pagans because they worshipped every kind of "god" except for YHWH. But yet, it was YHWH's will for the Gentile nations to receive His Salvation (Isaiah 49:6, 42:6). He told Abraham that through him all the nations of the earth would be blessed (Genesis 12:1-3). Early believing Jews didn't understand that this and at first proclaimed the Good News of the Messiah only to Jewish people. Consequently, the controversy in the First Century was not **if** it was Jewish to believe in Yeshua but whether Gentiles could be included without having to become Jewish (addressed by the Jerusalem council – Acts 15:1-31).

**Question:** Yeshua said He came NOT to abolish but to fulfill/establish/confirm (Matthew 5:17). He also said that until all has been accomplished, and heaven and earth have passed away, not one "jot or tittle"/the smallest letter or stroke would disappear from the Torah (Matthew 5:18). Has ALL been accomplished yet? Have heaven and earth passed away yet? If not, why are you ignoring Torah?

**Answer:** Since Yeshua said He did NOT come to abolish Torah, we MUST adhere to Torah! The Bible clearly shows that Yeshua was a Jew who did not come to abolish the faith of Judaism or the Torah, but to magnify, establish, and confirm it. And He said: *Matthew 5: 19 So whoever disobeys the least of these mitzvot (words/commands) and teaches others to do so will be called the least in the Kingdom of Heaven. But whoever obeys them and so teaches will be called great in the Kingdom of Heaven. 20 For I tell you that unless your righteousness is far greater than that of the Torah-teachers and P'rushim, you will certainly not enter the Kingdom of Heaven.*

**Question:** According to Joel 2:32 and Acts 2:21, those who are saved will do what?

**Answer:** They will call on the Name of YHWH. Not on Allah or Krishna or the Mahdi, or even "Jesus" because that's NOT His Name!

**Question:** The Bible in several places states that YHWH's Word is forever. Did "forever" end at the beginning of the "New Testament"?

**Answer:** No! Forever never ends, so why are Christians negating YHWH's Torah - His original divine teachings today?

*Psalm 119:89 "Forever, O Lord, Your word is settled in heaven."*

*Isaiah 59: 21 – "And as for Me," says ADONAI, "this is My covenant with them: my spirit, who rests on you, and my words which I put in your mouth will not depart from your*

191

*mouth, or from the mouth of your children, or from the mouth of your children's children, now or ever," says ADONAI.*

"Forever" hasn't come unless "everything has happened that must happen" and "heaven and earth have passed away" (Revelation 21:1). Has the heavenly Jerusalem already come down from heaven to the Earth (Revelation 21:2)? Has Satan already been punished and cast into the lake of fire? (Revelation 20:10.) Has the Great White Throne Judgment occurred already? (Revelation 20:11-12.) Has Yeshua already returned and established the Kingdom of God (Revelation 10:1-7 and 19:6, 11-16)? (Also see Isaiah 59:21 and 1 Chronicles 16:15.)

**Question:** Do you really believe that by ignoring Torah you are provoking the Jews to jealousy (Romans 11:11:12)? Do you think Jews are going to be jealous of pork and shrimp eating Christians who ignore the true Sabbath and the Biblical feasts, and are asking the Jews to give up the entire half of the Bible that contains the Torah which is our ONLY divine instructions on moral living?

**Answer:** YHWH used the Jews to spread the Word about Himself and His Son. If He hadn't "scattered the Jews into the nations" nobody would ever have heard of YHWH or Yeshua! Yet many supposed Christians openly hate the Jews and condemn Isra'el while supporting their enemies.

Believers are commanded to spread the Gospel to the entire world; this includes our Jewish brethren – yet Christians have killed millions of Jews and been responsible for persecuting them in one way or another for centuries. And now you want to give them a "New Testament" concussion by insisting "Jesus nailed to the cross" our Creator's DIVINE instructions and insist Jews are going to hell unless they start believing in Jesus?

You want to tell them that THEIR God – the God of Abraham, Isaac, and Jacob whom you also worship – has come in the form of a **man** they are supposed to worship, and that the man is more important than the Father and that he has abolished the Father's original teachings? You demand of the Jews that they throw away their Tanakh because you believe Jesus' death on the cross automatically negated ALL of God's original teachings? You want them to believe they should throw out the original God-breathed Word and adhere to "the other half" of the Bible in which the Apostle Paul said things that Christians have misunderstood, misinterpreted and misapplied as negating Torah? You want them to give up the idea of the YHWH-commanded seventh-day Sabbath and the Biblical feasts; the very feasts that Yeshua is STILL in the process of fulfilling?

To win the heart of a Jew, you must first remember that Yeshua was a Torah observant, seventh day Sabbath and Biblical feast-keeping, kosher **Jew**! You must also realize that the reason most Jews do not and cannot believe in Him is because their "spiritual eyes" have not yet been opened – in part because Christianity has not been presenting Yeshua in a Biblical light. YHWH Himself will open their eyes in due time – and He will use Torah observant Believers to help them see the Truth.

**Question:**   Christians insist that "the law" was "written on our hearts" (Jeremiah 31:33-34; Romans 10:4-8) and therefore, the "OT" no longer pertains to them.  How can you know what "the law" is, if you don't first study and learn to obey it?  Man is born into sin; he does not automatically know "right" from "wrong"– which is what Torah is all about.

**Answer:**   Let's view this from another standpoint: Unless we have read and understood the "Old Testament" how can we automatically KNOW what Torah says?  Yes, we have "the law"/Torah written on our hearts – however, this does not mean we have an automatic knowledge of it just because we are "saved".   It means we now have the **desire** for Torah!   We need to remember that the heart is the "seat of desire" as it is the battleground over which YHWH and Satan continually fight....

**Question:**   In Revelation 12:17, at whom is the Dragon enraged?

**Answer:**    Those who hold to the Testimony of Yeshua, AND obey His Commandments!

While all the questions comments contained in this book might come across as somewhat harsh, those who are truly seeking will understand and begin to adhere to YHWH's teachings.  Rather than to try to figure out ways to "get out of" being Torah observant, they will stop celebrating the pagan holidays of Christmas and Easter and start learning about GOD's appointed times. They will no longer settle for the "milk" they've been fed in their churches, and they will begin to hold themselves and their pastors accountable for teaching the Word of God according to the **whole** Word of God.

**Question:**    Is it okay to ignore God's commands, just because Jesus died on the cross?

**Answer:**    Please think very hard about that question, because I believe you will come to the conclusion that the answer is a resounding "NO!" It simply does not make any sense to insist that just because Jesus died, all of God's original teachings went out the window. It makes no sense to think the seventh day Sabbath which our Creator instituted and personally observed (Genesis 2:2) was changed to the first day, or that pork and shellfish somehow became "clean" just because Jesus died!

In Matthew 5:17 Jesus even said: *"Do **not** think that I came to abolish the Law or the Prophets; I did **not** come to abolish but to fulfill."* That indicates a beginning, not an ending or an "abolishing." If Yeshua didn't "abolish" then "fulfill" CANNOT mean "put an end to." As I've mentioned before, Torah is our **only** blueprint for moral, godly living. How could that have ended with the death of Yeshua?

Since Christians are believers in the God of Abraham, Isaac and Jacob, doesn't it stand to reason that His

195

Torah applies to ALL and not just "some"? Why would YHWH set down a separate set of laws for a certain group of people, especially since we see throughout the "Old Testament" that the "foreigners" and those who have chosen to attach themselves to Israel, are to do **exactly** as the Jews/Hebrews!

ALL believers have a duty to know and obey God's Torah! Once you know and understand Torah and the Tanach ("Old Testament"), the "New Testament" takes on a whole new meaning....

2420794